AF623556

WATER USER ASSOCIATIONS IN ANDHRA PRADESH

About the Author

With a background of Engineering and Political Economy, the author has published extensively on issues of water management. Widely travelled in the field areas as a researcher and development consultant, the author displays a remarkable ability to connect and analyze the disparate empirical observations at the grass-roots in the context of macro concerns of current water policy and practice. At present she is based at Hyderabad and works as an independent consultant.

About the Institute

Centre for Economic and Social Studies (CESS) has been recognised as a national institute for its role in the promotion of research and training. Its objectives are to conduct interdisciplinary research in analytical and applied areas of social sciences and to provide the Central and State Governments assistance by conducting various policy-related studies, systematic studies of resourse potential, examining measures for reducing poverty both at macro and micro levels. It also organises Seminars, Workshops and Lectures, and conducts Training Courses/Programmes for University and College Teachers and Public functionaries. CESS is instrumental in establishing fruitful contacts with other institutions and scholars engaged in social science research through collaborative research programmes to develop and enrich social science research. The Centre has been recognised as a Centre for advanced research by Dr. B. R. Ambedkar Open University and the Osmania University as well as by the University of Hyderabad for external registration of Ph.D. Programmes.

WATER USER ASSOCIATIONS IN ANDHRA PRADESH

Initial Feedback

JASVEEN JAIRATH

Foreword by

PROF. S. MAHENDRA DEV

Director, Centre for Economic and Social Studies, Hyderabad

Published for

CENTRE FOR ECONOMIC AND SOCIAL STUDIES, HYDERABAD

by

CONCEPT PUBLISHING COMPANY, NEW DELHI-110059

All Rights reserved. No part of this work may be reproduced, stored in a retrieval system, or transmitted in any form or by any means, electronic, mechanical photocoying, microfilming, recording or otherwise, without the prior written permission of the copyright owner and the publisher.

ISBN 81-7022-882-4

First Published 2001

© Centre for Economic and Social Studies, Hyderabad

Published and Printed by
Ashok Kumar Mittal
Concept Publishing Company
A/15-16, Commercial Block, Mohan Garden
New Delhi-110059 (India)

Phones: 5648039, 5649024
Fax: 091–(11)–5648053
Email: publishing@conceptpub.com

Foreword

Irrigation has been the key force behind agricultural development. Substantial public investment has been made for construction of large number of irrigation projects. The farmers have not derived full benefits from these projects because of inadequate maintenance and management. Participation in Irrigation Management (PIM) is considered as an important institutional arrangement for improving the operational efficiency and financial viability of irrigation systems. The aim of PIM is to reduce the sphere of responsibility of the government and encourage user groups to take over maintenance, management of water allocation, and collection of water rates. This is the best way of ensuring effective local management of irrigation. Recognising the importance of PIM, the state of Andhra Pradesh has made a pioneering move to create Water User Associations (WUAs) under the Andhra Pradesh Farmer's Management of Irrigation System's Act, 1997. The main objectives of the legislation were to provide legal backing for implementing measures to institutionalise the participation of irrigation users in the operation and maintenance of irrigation systems. Currently, around 10,000 WUAs are working in the state. The Andhra experiment of irrigation reforms is being watched with tremendous interest within and outside the country. However, a critical assessment of the experience must precede any attempt at emulation of the model.

In this study, Dr. Jasveen Jairath has made an initial assessment of the working of the PIM (Water user Associations) in Andhra Pradesh. The experience of WUAs in the state was studied by selecting a sample of areas irrigated by tanks and canals. Tanks were selected from the district of Ranga Reddy, while canal irrigated areas were selected from the command areas of Nagarjuna Sagar: Left Canal Project (NSPLC) and Sri Ram Sagar (SRSP) project. The field work was done in 1999. Specifically, the study examines the impact of PIM on the following issues:

(a) Efficiency of water use by reducing supply side inefficiencies,
(b) Increase in agricultural productivity,
(c) Financial viability of the irrigation systems,
(d) Institutional and managerial efficiency,
(e) Impact of PIM on Maintenance and Operation to become more user responsive and need based,
(f) PIM and variation in cost of irrigation to the water use,
(g) Impact of PIM to resolve head-tail and land based inequity in accessing water and facilitate conflict resolution.

One of the conclusions is that the work has been progressing well on physical structures (e.g. desilting). There has been an increase in the area irrigated due to PIM. The sustainability of WUAs depends on the financial viability of these associations. The author finds two main problems relating to working of the WUAs. One is that it does not address the question of equity in the distribution of water between head enders and tail enders. The second one is that the increase in area irrigated has been largely absorbed by rice cultivation. The author advocates that incentives have to be created to shift cropping pattern from rice to dry land crops. However, some more time has to be given to WUAs for addressing the issue of equity in sharing of water. There will be success stories and failure stories on the functioning of WUAs over time. One can learn from these experiences and rectify any deficiencies in the system.

The Centre is happy to bring this timely and comprehensive study on the critical issue of water management and hopes its findings will assist in formulating a balanced policy on the subject.

July, 2000

S. Mahendra Dev
Director,
Centre for Economic and Social Studies

Acknowledgements

Research for the study was carried out at the Centre for Economic and Social Studies, Hyderabad, during 1998-1999. The study support through a grant from Reserve Bank of India is gratefully acknowledged. I am very grateful to the support and encouragement provided by CESS for successfully completing my research work. I am deeply indebted to Professors C.H. Hanumantha Rao and M. Venkatramaiah whose constant encouragement, support, guidance and motivation was crucial for enriching and refining the work. Comments, suggestions and observations of the following have gone a long way towards sharpening and chiselling the outcome of the study and my own understanding of the subject—Prof. S. Mahendra Dev, Prof. A. Vaidyanathan, Prof. Krishnaji, Robert Chambers, Bhale Rao, Raymond Peter, P. K. Agarwal, Peter Mollinga, Satyanarain Singh, Ashok Gulati, Anil C. Shah and all the engineers of the irrigation department at the field level as well as the farmers.

The help and support on the logistics front provided by the irrigation department at the field level was invaluable, without which the study would not have been possible. The innumerable women and men farmers who spared their valuable time to share their perceptions with me have contributed beyond measure to developing my own insights towards understanding a very complex and critical issue. They were the books of learning that opened my eyes to the dynamic of social forces at a micro level – an education I could scarcely have acquired elsewhere.

Last but not the least, I would like to mention the deep appreciation of the administrative staff of CESS who were ever ready to provide whatever support was required at whatever time.

Notwithstanding the wide range of inputs as above, I accept full responsibility for the conclusions, errors, inconsistencies and shortcomings of the study.

JASVEEN JAIRATH

Contents

1

INTRODUCTION

PARTICIPATORY IRRIGATION MANAGEMENT (PIM)

The Concept, its Rationale and Benefits

PIM is essentially the participation of the users of irrigation in the decision making process of any matter relating to the creation and utilisation of irrigation potential. In addition it may also imply sharing of the actual responsibilities of execution, operation and maintenance, but within the context of some element of *control* over decisions. This is to be distinguished from a mere physical involvement in irrigation related activity without a concomitant capability to influence the pertinent decisions. While the former implies control by the users over irrigation development and utilisation, the latter connotes a subjection to the decisions of an alien authority– typically an irrigation bureaucracy in the case of large-scale surface irrigation systems.

Given the various forms of socio-technical processes of irrigation, equal diversity is observed in the extent and character of PIM. Depending on the nature of the activity in which users are involved, and the role of that activity in the total process of irrigation, participation can vary in kind and degree. For instance it can range from near total participation found in small-scale irrigation systems (e.g. dug wells, small tanks etc.) encompassing creation to operation and maintenance. On the other extreme, could be the participatory operation and maintenance (O&M) of the terminal points of a large-scale surface irrigation network of canals. The essential point about PIM is the *decentralised* character of management strategy applicable equally to large and small-scale irrigation systems. Participation of users at the level of decentralised units decreases the need for control typically required by a highly centralised management of irrigation systems—particularly the large ones. In so far as this implies the incorporation of the user viewpoint via participation it also implies a degree of democratic functioning. This is in stark contrast to the top down bureaucratic form of centralised management of most irrigation systems—whereby the users at the terminal point have to adjust their entire production schedule to the rigid and often unpredictable time frame of the irrigation supplied.

The critical contribution of PIM that enhances irrigational productivity derives from a better articulation of the constraints and limitations of suppliers with the needs/demands of water users. Participation of users acts as a channel of communication for conveying information about the concrete conditions of production (and in that context of irrigation also) to the relevant supplying agency such as the department of irrigation. Thus, facilitating a two-way communication, as opposed to the one way (top-down) typically observe in most existing large-scale systems. The probability of delivering an irrigation service suited to the specific needs of the local users is greatly enhanced. However, this feedback from the field to the top is an ongoing requirement, if the changes in the ground level situation are to be constantly reflected and incorporated in the provision of irrigation service. Of late there has been a growing realisation by the government and donor agencies that rupturing of this link with the field has been responsible for a large measure of mismatch between supply and use of irrigation. The heavy investment carried out in the creation of huge structures is thereby rendered partially infructuous.

The act of participation also involves an element of responsibility—of accountability—on the part of participants. Specially for the consequences of activity in which they are participating e.g. water distribution, water fee collection etc. As such the onus of ensuring an efficient use of water resources is partly transferred to the users. Having a stake in sustained and reliable availability of requisite water resource, the users in all likelihood would be motivated to honour this responsibility. Participation by users can, therefore, also contribute towards ensuring relevant, feasible and reliable irrigation.

Broadly, the major benefits of participation may be identified as follows:

1. Greater productivity,
2. Improved water distribution—in terms of equity and /or reliability,
3. Conflict resolution,
4. Greater local resource mobilisation for supporting innovative design/construction and O&M activities, and
5. Ecologically sustainable use of land and water resources.

India had launched an ambitious programme of irrigational development after independence. The successive Five-Year Plans bear evidence of the heavy investment sunk into the creation of large dams euphemistically called "temples of modern India" by Jawaharlal Nehru. These dams coupled with the extensive network of surface channels, led to the creation of thousands of hectares of irrigation potential. From the sixties onwards the emphasis shifted from major to medium and minor schemes, which gave further fillip to the creation of irrigation potential. However, notwithstanding the large investment, it was soon realised that the utilisation of the irrigation potential was not commensurate with the level of its creation. The gap—well acknowledged in official circles—was wide and glaring.

The situation at the grassroots was equally dismal. The efficiency of irrigation provided was very poor in terms of the quantum of water supplied and the control over the time and quantity of water by the actual users. Problems of water sharing among multiple users arising from their antagonistic interests further compromised the efficiency. In addition, the benefits were unequally shared. In totality, the conflict-ridden situation led to a dissipation of the available sources. The Command Area

Development (CADA) approach of the 70s and 80s also did not create the expected impact. The need to work towards optimal utilisation of the water resource was, therefore, acutely felt. In this context it was also realised and acknowledged that irrigation systems wherein the users had some degree of involvement in the functioning often performed better.

The above is not to suggest that participation *per se* can alleviate all the causes of sub-optimal operation of irrigation systems. Certainly structural and technical *upstream problems* can limit (and in some cases even discourage) the realisation of potential benefits of participatory management. However, given the typical observation of poor maintenance, water stealing, wasteful cultivation practices, etc., experienced at the field level, enlisting farmers' cooperation can go a long way towards improving system performance.[1]

While the concept of PIM has gained widespread acceptability within government, donor agencies and NGO circles, the evidence on its actual practice points to a mixed experience.[2] Broadly two patterns of implementing PIM have been identified (WAU, 1990)—top down and bottom up approaches. "Well known examples of top down approaches in India include among others (a) turnover of O&M responsibilities to pipe committees in Sri Ram Sagar Project, Andhra Pradesh (Pathak, 1991), (b) turnover of O&M responsibilities to minor level organisations in Mula and Jaikwadi Projects, Maharashtra (Pathak, 1991) (c) turnover of tubewells to village panchayat samitis under the West Bengal Irrigation Research Project (Bandhopadhayay, 1992), and (d) turnover of water distribution to the Mohini Water Distribution Cooperative Society in the Ukai-Kakrapar System in Gujarat (Pathak)........examples of bottom up turnover .... (a) takeover of farmers of management of the Pillaging Distributary of the Sone System in Bihar (Srivastava and Brewer, 1994), (b) the direct involvement of farmer created organizations in management of parts of the Tambaraparani command in Tamil Nadu (Pundarikanthan *et al.*, 1992) and in Tughabhadra System in Andhra Pradesh (Wade, 1987) etc." (Brewer *et al.*, 1998).

In this context the PIM strategy in AP represents a top down approach initiated and implemented by the government and encompassing the entire gamut of public irrigation works. The scale of the programme and the political, financial, legal and administrative backing it has received from the state represents an attempt to 'catch the bull by the horns' and is very laudable indeed. However, due to the absence of grassroot interventions to complement the initiative from above, there is the likelihood of weak representation of the general body of water users in the formal institutions of Water User Organisations. In particular of that section of cultivators who are marginalized as a matter of routine by the working out of political and economic forces at the local level. This may partly neutralise the participatory character of these institutions and adversely influence their sustainability and effectiveness for realising efficient and equitable water use. However, purely bottom up initiatives are also very often limited in scale and lack the politico-administrative backing required for horizontal diffusion of the development benefits. An effective integration of the interventions from both ends appears desirable for generating a genuine and vibrant participation of not only users but also other stakeholders for common management of a natural resource such as water.

PIM in AP

AP has three major rivers Krishna, Godavary and Pennar, whose dependable flows are 2746 TMC of water, out of which 1846 TMC has been tapped for irrigation, creating an irrigation potential of 4.8 million hectares under major and medium projects. Out of this only 2.84 million hectares is being irrigated, reflecting a gap of about 41%. "Existing usage of water is inefficient, wasteful, inequitable with tail end deprivation being almost universal. Further, widespread deterioration of infrastructure with little or no participation of farmers has aggravated the low utilisation of water of irrigation commands". (Says the note on the AP farmers' management of irrigation systems Act of 1997, Irrigation Department, Government of AP). The area irrigated under some of the major and medium projects was shrinking, inspite of secular increase in capital expenditure (corrected for inflation) and increasing M&O expenses. Finally, the financial returns to the investment in irrigation were very poor due to low rates of water cess and low rates of fee collection. That the performance of irrigation projects in AP on technological, managerial and financial fronts was very poor—was well recognised and acknowledged within the government circles.

Within this backdrop—The AP Farmers Management of Irrigation Systems Act was passed in the Legislative Assembly on 27-3-1997. The main objectives of the legislation were to provide a legal backing for implementing measures to institutionalise the participation of irrigation users in the operation and maintenance of irrigation systems. That is: (1) ensuring equitable and reliable supplies, (2) bridge the gap between irrigation potential created and utilised through preparation of suitable operation plans, (3) bring about social audit and water audit in irrigation, (4) enable the department to withdraw from M & O, and concentrate on the reservoir management and development of new systems.

The thrust was on decentralising irrigation management—thereby, according a greater responsibility as well as greater powers to bodies comprising elected representatives of water users. Involvement and control by the users at the local level, it was believed, would constitute an incentive to improve operational performance. The entire exercise would lead to improvement in quality and cost efficiency of irrigation management leading to increased profitability of irrigated agriculture—often inspite of increased cost of irrigation to the user. The process was perceived to be a cost saving venture for the government wherein the released resources could be used for raising investment in irrigation elsewhere or on the main system.

The proposals for operationalising the above ideas envisaged the creation of an institutional structure of irrigation water users with Water User Associations as its basic elements. Main features of these proposals, as spelt out in the Act, may be summarised as follows:

1. The Act is applicable to all irrigation schemes Major, Medium and Minor except those under Panchayat Raj Institutions and all minor bodies in the Scheduled areas of AP

2. Every irrigation project would be divided into convenient areas of operation of the project and distributary committees, and water user associations at the primary level. The delineation of the areas would be done on a hydraulic basis, which are administratively and functionally viable. Each of the farmers organisations has to be divided into even number of territorial constituencies within a Water Users' Association as follows:

3. *For Major and Medium Projects:*

(a) Upto 1000 ha.	4	Constituencies
(b) From 1001 – 1500 ha.	6	Constituencies
(c) From 1501 – 2000 ha	8	Constituencies
(d) More than 2000 ha	10	Constituencies

For Minor Projects :

(a) Upto 200 ha.	4	Constituencies
(b) From 201 – 400 ha	6	Constituencies
(c) From 401 – 600 ha	8	Constituencies
(d) From 600 – 2000 ha	10	Constituencies

4. Depending on the type of irrigation scheme, there may be single, two or three-tier system of associations/committees. Each Assistant Engineer (AE) will be in-charge of a maximum of 10,000 acres and Deputy Executive Engineer will handle 40-50,000 acres.

5. *Water User Associations:* These are the primary organisational units of irrigation water users. Each irrigation scheme may comprise one or more WUAs. While medium and minor projects could comprise of a single WUA, depending on the ayacut, the major projects could be divided into a few hundred WUAs, depending on the spread of the ayacut and the spatial

distribution of distributaries. These primary units of water users shall regulate and distribute water within its command area. The total area of operation of a WUA will be divided into 4-10 constituencies, depending on its command area. Each constituency shall elect a member of the managing committee of the WUA and shall directly elect the President of the WUA as well.

6. *Distributary Committee (DC):* A group of WUAs under a distributary or a group of small distributaries comprises a DC. The Presidents of all WUAs under a distributary in a DC are members of a DC. Together they are to select the members of the managing committee and the DC President, who will be incharge of the distributary related matters.
7. *Project Committees:* These are apex bodies concerned with the management and distribution of water in the command of major and medium projects. All the DC Presidents will be members of the PC. The entire project command is to be divided into 7-11 constituencies to ensure adequate representation. The PC will elect a President and 7–11 managing committee members from each constituency.
8. *Apex Committee:* An apex committee chaired by the minister of major and medium projects shall be constituted to formulate broad policy guidelines for the various committees in its command and act as the final decision making body for resolving disputes.
9. *Membership of WUAs:* All landholders within localised/ authorised area including titleholders, tenants and whose names are found in Record of Rights shall be members of WUA with voting rights. All other water users either from non-localised areas or users for non-agricultural purposes will also be co-opted as members but without voting rights.
10. *Functions of these organizations:* These organisations are charged with the following main functions:

    (a) Preparation of operational plans at the beginning of each season,

(b) Prepare a panel of auditors for auditing accounts,
(c) Maintain an inventory of irrigation system within its command (i.e. wells, borewells, tanks etc.),
(d) Maintenance of records, accounts, list of members and implementing the decisions of the higher committees,
(e) To prepare the maintenance plan of the distributary and drainage system of the irrigation project within its command and execute local maintenance works,
(f) Social audit and water budgeting,
(g) Conflict resolution,
(h) Resource mobilisation.

11. *Resources of these organisations*

(a) Government grants as a share of water fee collected,
(b) Development grants,
(c) Loans raised from any scheduled or cooperative banks,
(d) Income from any sources attached to the irrigation sources,
(e) Levy or special tax for taking up specific works as agreed upon by general body.

12. Significant features of the proposals

(a) The *right to recall* of the president if the general body members are dissatisfied is indeed novel. Provisions have been made for recall of the president if there is a one-third majority of the general body members,
(b) Membership is based only on the *fact* of owning or cultivating land in the authorised command of the WUA and not on the *extent* of the land owned,
(c) Control over water use is in the hands of localised irrigation water users at the expense of non-irrigation users of water,
(d) The landless (which includes women since typically they are not the legal owners of family land) are excluded from any involvement in water management in the area. The high levels of public investment in irrigation which has

an impact on the entire community—directly and indirectly—focuses on a fraction of the population i.e. those who practice irrigated agriculture.

Following these proposals and passing of the Act in 1997, elections for nearly 10,000 WUAs were held on 17th June, 1997 (one President and Technical constituency members as per the WUA command) as shown in Tables 1.1 & 1.2 and Map 1.1. Subsequent to the elections, extended training was provided to government officers and Presidents of WUAs to sensitise them about PIM—its features and necessity. Training programme for all the WUA Presidents and members was conducted in June 1999 at a cost of Rs. 2.5 crores (DIPR, 1999). As a result of the reforms 22,171 works at a cost of Rs. 107 crores have been taken up and completed (DIPR, 1999). See also Table 1.3 below for a detail of financial resources expended and works completed during the second year. During the first year activities taken up in canal irrigated areas took the form of silt clearance of channels, followed by strengthening of embankments, small repairs of pipe outlets and drop structures, plugging of breaches etc. The emphasis during the second year has shifted to the fixing of shutters at the various off take points. This is significant, as existence of shutters is a precondition of any attempts to institute water regulation. The farmers also singularly emphasised this during the fieldwork as discussed later. Technical systems of water regulation are a necessary although not a sufficient condition, for implementing any rules of water distribution within water users at the field level and within distributaries at the main system level. The ayacutdars, particularly at the tail end were acutely conscious of this.

As of now there exist hardly any systematic method of equal water sharing. The water is continuously flowing in all the channels (depending on the quantum of water releases at the head of the system) throughout the irrigation season. As such, the ease of water availability to a user is in proportion to the distance of his land from the head of the irrigation system. Head refers to head of the system, head of the distributary and head of the minor. Similarly, tail end refers to the end of a channel—main canal,

Map. 1.1: Spread of water user organisations in Districts (A.P.)

TABLE 1.1: The Number of Water User Associations in the State On 10-12-1998

Sl. No.	Name of the District	MAJOR		MEDIUM	MINOR	Total WUAs
		WUAs	DCs	WUAs	WUAs	
1.	Adilabad	61	4	18	211	290
2.	Karimnagar	249	18	10	520	779
3.	Nizamabad	78	11	6	231	315
4.	Nalgonda	94	6	45	534	673
5.	Warangal	29	2	19	646	694
6.	Khammam	51	7	7	178	236
7.	Mahabubnagar	39	3	39	466	544
8.	Medak	-	-	12	563	575
9.	Ranga Reddy	-	-	2	165	167
10.	Srikakulam	37	9	31	448	516
11.	Vijayanagaram	-	-	22	429	429
12.	Visakhapatnam	28	5	19	363	410
13.	East Godavary	108	9	12	232	352
14.	West Godavary	69	5	9	220	298
15.	Krishna	191	21	9	265	485
16.	Guntur	241	19	8	74	323
17.	Prakasam	130	13	6	345	481
18.	Nellore	70	14	36	593	69
19.	Chittoor	-	-	89	644	644
20.	Ananthapur	48	5	7	276	331
21.	Kurnool	115	15	21	151	287
22.	Cuddapah	88	8	8	270	366
	Total	1726	174	435	7824	9985

Source: CADA, Irrigation Department, GOAP, Hyderabad.

TABLE 1.2: Abstract of WUAs in the State, 1998

Projects	*WUAs Already Formed*			WUAs to be elected	Total
	Unanimous	Elected	Total		
Major	649	1,077	1,726	30	1,756
Medium	118	317	435	7	442
Minor	4,714	3,110	7,824	270	8,094
Total	5,489	4,504	9,985	307	10,292

distributary and minor. The water availability reduces progressively as you proceed towards the tail of a channel. The tail end of a minor at the tail of a tail end distributary will bear the accumulated losses en route. Similarly, it is possible that the tail end of a head end distributary may get plenty of water while the head end of a tail end distributary gets meagre or uncertain supplies.

In principle, the water distribution according to the Act is supposed to be on per acre basis with the cropping pattern left entirely to choice of the farmer. However, as of date, the distribution principal in operation was "first come first serve"—'come' in the sense of location of the farmer's plot of land from the source of water. The traditional discrimination based on locational disadvantage is very much extant. Compounded on that is the disadvantage of smaller size of landholding of majority of the farmers. While there is a direct disadvantage of smallholdings accessing water during a stipulated time as water obtained in lump sum has lower per unit losses during use compared to its distribution in smaller quantities. The indirect disadvantage is the poor access to non-water complementary inputs for production which are typically a function of the resource position of the cultivator as represented roughly by his land size. These inputs influence the productivity of available irrigation water.

Although the DCs did have meetings with the respective irrigation department personnel on the availability of water in the reservoir and the possibility of releases during the ensuing season,

TABLE 1.3: District Wise Programme and Progress of Works during 1999-2000

Grand Total for all districts	Fund Sanctioned in Rs.	Works Programmed (1998)		Works Sanctioned		Agreements Concluded		Works Grounded		Amount Paid Rs. Lakh	Works Completed	
	Lakhs (1998)	No.	Value Rs. Lakhs	No.	Value in Rs. Lakhs	No.	Value in Rs. Lakhs	No.	Value in Rs. Lakhs		No.	Value in Rs. Lakhs
1	2	3	4	5	6	7	8	·9	10	11	12	13
WUAs	12471.58	15573	10695.66	12440	8474.79	6670	4915	4865	3472.40	809.24	72	158.44
District Committees	6522.44	2092	5452.50	1527	4376.99	848	2633.37	596	1751.71	459.89	1	0.69
Project Committees	19572.51	668	13833.83	451	11651.57	80	2808.81	41	1699.61	0.00	1	26.00
Total	38566.53	18333	29981.99	14418	24503.35	7598	10357.78	5502	6923.72	1269.13	74	185.13

Source: DIPR, Government of Andhra Pradesh.

this could only be for information. It did not reflect a greater control over the releases or distribution—however, it did create the possibility of farmers planning their production pattern according to the expected supplies. But in the absence of an effective communication system, it is unlikely that such information would reach to the general body of farmers for them to respond by taking preemptive action. There was thus, very little that is in evidence on redressing the imbalance on equity front—both the head–tail and land based —regarding changes in distribution of water due to formation of WUAs in the state.

Context and Strategy of PIM in AP

One of the major arguments advanced for PIM was that it would reduce the work burden on the government department that could eventually be reflected in reduced workforce and greater concentration on the main system and developing new projects for extending irrigation services to a wider area. The evidence regarding the work burden was precisely opposite—nearly all the officers who were interviewed in the field and head offices (irrigation and local administration) in the research area, maintained the heavy work load as a result of initiating the PIM programme in AP—the entire process of preparation for election, its conduct, the trainings, holding of three to four *Sadassus*[3] of all the presidents of WUAs and one meeting of the presidents of DCs, guiding the WUAs on the preparation of financial estimates of the physical works proposed by them, technical guidance for the execution of these works, etc. along with the routine work being done by the field level staff e.g. "Laskars" and works inspectors to monitor water delivery in the channels. However the increased workload of the department is likely to be of a temporary nature evident during the first phase of transition. Eventually it is expected to decline as the latter work is envisaged to be taken up by the WUAs any way they choose—either by hiring their own staff or sharing duties among themselves as mutually agreed upon. As of date, the progress on this front is stalled inspite of readiness by the government to hand over the field staff to the WUAs, due to the resistance on the part of the field staff to be under the control of the WUAs and to be accountable to them. They have gone to the Court and have obtained a stay on the government order to this effect. In fact, the government was also ready to pay the salaries of the staff. The question was of *control and accountability*–which was resisted by the lower rung of the irrigation department. This accountability of nodal officers (Competent Authority–who are like "single windows" for the WUAs to contact the department for any matter relating to water management in their area) also constitutes an integral part of the new legislation.[4] Creation of these institutions has succeeded in providing a forum for expression of the collective demands, problems and concerns and channelling the communication to the government in a systematic manner. In place of anarchy, confusion, and randomness—there is a relative order in getting the message across. Most farmers during field survey preferred to deal with the WUA office bearers rather than the Irrigation department officials, as was the case formerly. Whatever reservation the individual farmers may have had regarding the degree of effectiveness of the WUAs, they were unanimous in welcoming the establishment of these organisations. While personal patronage seemed to be the only avenue for getting a hearing at the higher echelons earlier—now there did exist institutions, manned by office bearers, where a relatively anonymous farmer could go for redressing his water related difficulties. This was corroborated by farmer responses in the field as discussed below.

The role of WUAs as an effective and organised link between the irrigation agency and the water user representatives depends however, on the degree of awareness among the farmers regarding the provisions of PIM. There is a strong case for investing in interventions geared to raising the awareness level of women and men farmers regarding the salient features of the initiatives taken by the state to enlist a greater participation of water users in the management of the irrigation systems. As a first step, the general body of water users needs to be made aware of their entitlements as well as their responsibilities.[5]

Organisation of elections by the Irrigation Department for

the formation of 10,000 WUAs on one single day for the entire state was a stupendous task. Smooth and fair conduct of elections by irrigation department and the local administration was commendable for its organisation, planning and execution. Nearly all the farmers surveyed in the field were satisfied with the mode of conducting elections. Later, we illustrate the effort, thinking and detailed planning that went into making the event a success. The sheer scale of elections and the fact that they were conducted for the first time is indicative of the political will to ground the programme.

Although turnout during the elections to the WUAs was significant, the degree of awareness about the programme varied across systems.[6] It is clear that a large part of the motivation to actively participate in the WUA is rooted in the funds being routed to these base units for carrying out the maintenance activities.[7] This raises the question of long run viability of WUAs once this source of funds dries up. Although the water fees has been increased by the government by more than 100% (from Rs. 40 per acre for wet crop to Rs. 200 per acre) there is yet no evidence of *increased collections* due to higher number of water users paying their fees and at the new rates which is the critical requirement.[8] Secondly, the fee continues to be collected by the revenue department according to their assessment of the area irrigated. The latter is usually at variance with the assessment of area irrigated by the irrigation department, as discussed below. This has serious implications for financial returns from irrigation projects, which has critical implications for sustainability of the WUAs. It has been reported that the revenue department has an interest in suppressing the area irrigated. This adversely affects the revenue on account of water charges received by the treasury. Higher water fees can contribute to the financial self-reliance of the WUAs only if it is combined with higher rates of fee collection. Financial autonomy and self-sufficiency, therefore, appear to be problematic.

As a result of instituting WUAs, irrigated acreage has shown a distinct and sharp increase in certain commands of major and medium projects. An official release by the Irrigation Minister noted that 5.12 lac acres of ayacut has been *additionally* brought under cultivation as a result of better maintenance work due to the reforms. The state has an ayacut gap of 15 lac acres. Therefore, nearly 10 lac additional gap had to be bridged. In all 23,011 works had been completed by March 1999 at a cost of rupees 135 crore. Paddy production had gone up by 10% and yield had increased from 30-35 bags per acre to 40-45 bags per acre. (TH, 1999). As we will argue below these figures are clearly exaggerated. Field observations, though limited to a small sample, do not indicate any changes to warrant the increase in productivity claimed above.

According to the recent statement by the Irrigation Minister, the maximum gap in irrigation potential bridged was in respect of SRSP project where irrigation potential created was 6,59,000 acres, average area irrigated during past three years was 1,15,000 acres and ayacut transplanted in the current year was 3,66,000 acres. Next came the Nizamsagar project with gap bridged being 74,000 acres, irrigation potential created being 23,000 acres, average ayacut irrigated during the past three years being 1,14,000 acres and ayacut transplanted during this season was 1,85,000 acres. A total of 17,000 acres of ayacut was bridged under Vamsadhara project, 50,000 acres under NSP-LC, 53,000 acres under NSP-RC, 10,000 acres under Tunghabhadra High Level Canal, 11,000 acres under Low Level Canal, 2,000 acres under Rajolibandh Diversion Scheme, and 23,000 acres under Kurnool Cuddapah Canal (Ministers Statement, 1998).

However, field visits indicate that the reported increase in irrigated area has to be interpreted cautiously. While it is true that physical works like desilting and clearing of irrigation channels has led to improved water flow–the actual number of wettings received and by what extent of the area, cannot be directly inferred from the above. There is a tendency for the official statistics to over state the area irrigated.

Field data analysis points to the fact that organisation of WUAs and the limited increase in water availability as a result of repair and rehabilitation of channels does not seem to have had much impact on the nature of cropping pattern and the level of physical yields of the crops. There has been an increase in area irrigated which has largely been absorbed by rice cultivation. To that extent cropping pattern has shifted to a higher proportion of area devoted to rice. Rice continues to be the major consumer of irrigation waters wherever feasible, such as at head reach areas. Downstream farmers use whatever proportion of water supplies that are left over for the usual irrigated dry crops such as maize, jowar, bajra, etc.

Although yield increase has also been claimed during the post reform period, it is highly suspect. Even, if increase in rice yield, which can be used as a proxy to assess the overall yield impact, is accepted, it is difficult to attribute it to the reform process in the same way as increase in irrigated acreage. Yield increase is the net outcome of multiple influences ranging from climatic factors to use of fertilisers, pesticides and controlled water application. In this context, it has to be borne in mind that 1997-99 were relatively good rainfall years. It is probably too early to hypothesize on the yield impact of reforms, which can be borne out as a result of changes in agricultural technology and/or practices that are made possible by the institution of irrigation reforms. Appropriate methodology for attributing yield changes to improvements in water management has to be evolved by netting out the impact of other secularly changing factors. As yet there is no evidence of, for instance, increasing per acre use of fertilizer, which is facilitated by requisite and assured irrigation. This is also corroborated by field observations.

NOTES

1. See Mollinga (1999) for a recent, serious and comprehensive case study of the dynamics of surface irrigation at the field level.
2. See Vermillion (1997) for a comprehensive review of PIM strategy all over the world and Meinzen-Dick (1997) with reference to India.
3. Gathering held for getting a feedback on the progress of reforms.
4. There have been instances of the farmers complaining about the negligence or uncooperative attitude of the concerned government officer and putting pressure for initiating action against him and succeeding.

5. This point is also emphasised by Vaidyanathan (1998).
6. Out of the 54 farmers interviewed in NSP-LC command area only 5 knew the name of the President of their WUA, 3 knew the name of their TC member. Women farmers—even land owning and cultivating small women farmers had little awareness regarding the whole programme. Hardly any general body meetings had been conducted in this area. Even the awareness of TC members regarding their role, responsibility and the three-tier structure of which they were a part was very poor. Most of these WUAs were single person dominated (i.e. the president) units. In the SRSP command area however, the situation was better. Out of 50 farmers interviewed from SRSP area16 knew the name of the WUA president and 10 knew the names of their TC member. Nearly 30% of the farmers mentioned that at least two general body meetings had been held so far, with a participation of more than 50%. There were more women TC members—and even a case of a very effective woman president as discussed later.
7. A total of Rs. 200 per acre was given to WUAs during 1998-99—inclusive of Rs. 100 per acre to WUAs and Rs. 100 given to DCs.
8. See also Vaidyanathan (1998) in this context.

2

RESEARCH MANDATE

The experience of PIM in the state of Andhra Pradesh was proposed to be studied by selecting a sample of areas irrigated by canals and tanks respectively. Tanks were selected from the district of Ranga Reddy, while canal irrigated areas were selected from among the command areas of Nagarjuna Sagar: Left Canal Project (NSPLC) and Sri Ram Sagar (SRSP) Project. The latter are two of the major projects of the state, and the experience of PIM therein would be quite representative of the state.

Five tanks from RR district were selected for detailed study to assess the impact of transfer of irrigation management to the water users. The district falls in the dry belt of Telangana region with an average rainfall of 300-400 mm. Main features of these tanks are shown in Table 2.1. Major crops grown under these tanks are Rice, Jowar, Maize and vegetables. Growth of deep-rooted plants such as *Juliflora trees* on the bed tanks[1], collection of silt and weak embankments are the main problems of the tanks, apart from the constraint of being rain dependent for source of water. Hence the inherent uncertainty of total quantum of water available. Some tanks are recharged by supplemental flows from the canal channels with relatively higher dependability.

Canal irrigated areas were selected from among the distributaries of NSP-LC project under the Myralgudda Circle (Wazeerabagh Distributary–WD) which lie in Nalgonda district and are in the upper range of the middle of the Left Canal of NSP. The average rainfall in the area is 400 mm. The land holding of farmers in the area varies from one to twenty acres. The major

TABLE 2.1 : Specification of Tanks and Feedback
(Ranga Reddy District)

Tank No.	Tank Name	Mandal	Ayacut acres	General Body No.	Amount spent on repairs after PIM (Rs.)	WUA office bearers No.	Source of funds	Works under-taken	Changes after PIM	Problems with PIM*	How cope with water scarcity
1.	Yebbanoor	Dharur	126	89	75,200/-	5	Govt.	Improv-ment of canals for water conveya-nce e.g. desilting, repairs of brea-ches etc.	Increase of area irrigated	Nil	By better manag-ement
2.	Parakrao Katwa	Dharur	350	134	501,000/-	5	Govt.			-	
3.	Mondikunta	Dharur	270	175	427,400/-	5	Govt.			-	
4.	Ayyammacher Utekullapally	Momin Pet	279	371	385,800/-	5	Govt.			-	
5.	Peddacheru Enkathalla	Momin Pet	324	247	414,800/-	5	Govt.			-	

Source: Division Office, Minor Irrigation, Vikharabad.

crops grown are rice, chillies, cotton and maize.

The second area under canal irrigation (under distributary D-89) was selected from the distributaries upstream of the LMD project under SRSP, under the LMD Circle of SRSP at Karimnagar. This area also lies in the upper end of middle reaches of the system. The size of land holding varies from one to twenty acres. The major crops grown are rice, maize, green gram, jowar and cotton.

Methodology of Data Collection

Primary level data was collected by fieldwork in the research areas through open-ended schedules administered to a stratified sample of members of the general body of WUAs as well as office bearers of WUAs in the region. Care was taken to select water users from tail, middle and head of minors, which were selected from tail, middle and head of the distributaries in the middle reach of both the systems. In addition, farmers were interviewed from head, middle and tail reaches of tanks. Users were selected from among large, medium and small farmers at each nodal point. Thus, 27 farmers from among 9 WUAs under Wazeerabagh Distributary (WD), 27 from among 6 WUAs under D-89 distributary under SRSP project, and 45 from among 5 WUAs under the tanks were interviewed. The WUAs under canal distributaries were selected from head, middle and tail areas as noted above. Therefore, a total of 99 (27+27+45) farmers were interviewed for collecting data on the impact of PIM on experience of the users as conditioned by their location on the irrigation system and their economic status as indicated by their land holding as above. In addition quick surveys of random sample of water users in the field areas were undertaken to get a feedback on farmer responses to PIM and for a social background of the WUA presidents. Illustrative data on cost of production of farmers at head, middle and tail were collected. Interviews were also held with the office bearers of WUAs as well as those excluded from the PIM programme e.g. the women. Meetings and discussions with the government officers, from the head office to the field level, were held to get insights regarding the qualitative aspects and secondary data collection. Participation in the state level *Sadassus* of WUA presidents, TC members and DC presidents were also used as opportunities to get a quick feedback on the perception of the various stakeholders regarding the entire programme. Data from the general body members was collected broadly on the following issues:

1. Changes in the availability of water, its timeliness and certainty,
2. Changes in the physical system of water supply and maintenance,
3. Changes in cropping pattern, intensity and crop yields as a result of WUA formation,
4. Changes in cost of water to the user and the ability to pay for it,
5. Changes in their relationship with the department and the nature of these,
6. Changes in conflict resolution the constraints experienced towards more effective implementation of PIM programme and their suggestions for carrying forward the process,
7. Finally, their awareness about the programme and the extent of their participation in its activities such as attending meetings or knowledge of the decisions taken at WUA or DC managing committee or taking decisions or solving problems of water allocation.

Data from secondary sources was collected for recent years on cropping pattern as wet and ID (irrigated dry) crop acreage, under the selected distributaries from the local irrigation department as well as the revenue department. These are the two sources where data is recorded independently but does'nt usually tally. The revenue department has a tendency to under-report the area irrigated which results in a loss of revenue to the irrigation department—not due to non-payment of the fees by the users but due to its leakage. The water releases at the distributary head were collected from the monitoring unit of the irrigation department. The financial data on the expenses for M & O, physical works done, water fees and the changes therein, and utilisation of funds for maintenance was all collected from the department.

Questions Explored

The following issues are proposed to be examined through the study for their possible policy implications:

1. Implementation of PIM programme will increase efficiency of water use. PIM will reduce supply side inefficiencies through effective grounding of technical works for rehabilitation of the main system and concurrent streamlining of the terminal channels by the initiatives undertaken by WUAs and DCs,
2. PIM and increase in agricultural productivity—increase of irrigated acreage, cropping intensity, physical yields and changes in cropping pattern towards efficient water consumption,
3. PIM and financial viability of the irrigation system—i.e. that it will ensure financial self-sufficiency, reduction of subsidies, financial transparency, higher collection of higher rate of irrigation fee,
4. PIM's capacity to engender institutional and managerial efficiency,
5. The impact of PIM on M & O to become more user responsive and need based—its nature, extent, timely execution and quality to show a marked improvement,
6. PIM and variation in cost of irrigation to the water user,
7. Impact of PIM to resolve head-tail and land based inequity in accessing water and facilitating conflict resolution.

NOTES

1. These plants have prolific growth and are very difficult to be uprooted, requiring mechanised extraction, which is expensive. However, the IB does not approve the budgets submitted for using WUA funds for certain tanks in Mahabubnagar district. The department policy was to expect the works to be undertaken by 'shramadan' or voluntary labour. This was unrealistic given the poor grassroot mobilization.

3

PIM AND WATER DISTRIBUTION CUM REGULATION

Control and regulation of water supply to individual users constitutes the main challenge for most public irrigation projects. One of the primary motivations for introducing PIM in the state of AP was to ensure equitable water distribution by instituting systems and rules of water distribution under major, medium and minor irrigation. Given the total quantum of water available, as determined by natural climatic factors, the time spread and volume of water available to users depends on the technological system and rules of water distribution. Typically water control is affected at four major points on the irrigation system.

First, it is at the stage of release of water from the reservoir. This is consequent on the decisions of the irrigation agency (the department) that manages the entire system, in accordance with criteria agreed upon depending on the priorities of the governing institutions. Technologically and managerially this does not present much of a problem. The next point of control is at the offtake points from the main canal. Here too installing control structures to regulate flow into different channels (distributaries) is relatively unproblematic as it remains under the control of the irrigation department. Tampering of structures by water users at this point has been the typical experience in the past, specially during low rainfall years. Once damaged their repair is taken up, if at all, after considerable time lag, during which the system continues to decay. It is not surprising, therefore, that repair of the offtake points on the main system has been a major thrust of activity. Further downstream, there is another set of channels (minors) which take off from these distributaries. Some control mechanisms at the head (take off points) of these minors are also provided. Finally pipe outlets are provided on these minors, which let out water to the field channels. These outlets are usually free flow outlets without any control mechanism. The individual water users access water by cutting openings on the field channels to allow water flow to their fields. Water use beyond this point is entirely under the control of the users. Control of water at the first and the last points does not lie within the domain of the reforms. Releases from the reservoir are no doubt subject to the expected demand based on the cropping pattern of the eventual water users. However, technological and managerial control remains under one agency, without any coordination problems experienced further downstream[1]. Neither are there any such impediments at the lowest level of the system as it is entirely under the domain of the individual user. It is mainly at the level of the offtake from the distributaries and to some extent from the main canal, that control of water distribution constitutes the problem area.

Technical structures like shutters had been installed at these points during the initial stages for controlling the flow into these inlets. The flow could be reduced or totally cut off depending on the water available and the requirements of equal distribution within the command areas. This was done through instituting a system of rotation of water supply, which means a sequential delivery of water to different channels in a predetermined order as opposed to simultaneous supply to all the channels taking off from a parent canal. While the latter could be feasible during surplus water availability, the former was a means of coping up with water scarcity, whereby allocations during lean period, would be reduced in equal proportion between entire command. Institutional functioning of the rotation system however, requires complementary technical function of the control structures. Tampering with the shutters, offtake structures etc. has been the observed pattern of user behaviour in the past, which has seriously jeopardised the efficacy of attempts to regulate water distribution.

Unauthorised withdrawals of water by upstream farmers using engines for pumping water, further accentuate the unequal distribution, which is to some extent inbuilt in the delivery system due to increased losses en route. This has resulted in continuation of the head tail discrimination in access to irrigation water from public sources—due to systemic and technical features as well as the violations of rules of water distribution.

Evidence from the Field

Control Structures

The existing method of water regulation and distribution, as originally planned, entailed an assessment of the water availability in the reservoir at the beginning of each cropping season, for NSP, SRSP canal projects and tanks. This determined the water releases during the season in the main canal. Flow in the main canal continued throughout the season (usually 3 to 4 months). Flow for Kharif starts in July and ends in December. For Rabi season it starts from January to April–May of the following year. April to July is called the closure period during which most of the major repair and maintenance works are carried out. Water was distributed to the command areas by means of the distributaries. Shutters had been installed at these offtake points as per the original project design (both for NSP and SRSP). The purpose of the shutters was to control the flow of water to different areas by deliberate design as prioritised at the beginning of the season. However, most of these shutters had been tampered with or damaged. There is thus, no effective control mechanism for directing the flow of water on a need basis. The head reach farmers of both the main canal and distributaries first appropriate as much water as they require and only the left over flows downstream. This leads to the typical problem of water scarcity at the tail end areas even when there is surplus water available to the head reach farmers. This led to an ironic situation of the head reach farmers taking two crops of rice during a year (1998-99) while the tail end farmers had severe problems in raising low water consumption crops i.e. cotton, chillies, etc. (see the following section on PIM and agricultural production). Line diagram (Fig. 3.1) of one of the distributaries in the sample areas show the dysfunctional state of the control structures before PIM on D-89. Similar story was repeated for WD. Out of 60 shutters installed at the beginning, none were functioning, and 36 were reconstructed as offtake sluices with shutters. In the NSP area control structures have been installed during the canal closure period of 1999 till the middle reaches of distributary. The same is contemplated for SRSP area in the following season. Demand from areas under tank irrigation for installation of sluices, repair of shutters etc. was forth coming. The initial financial allocation had been used more for clearance of silt and repair of some feeder channels. This demand for improved control mechanisms is also reflected in the responses of the farmers surveyed during fieldwork on the changes in the water availability after formation of WUAs. (See Table 3.1) 85% of the sample farmers recommended the installation of shutters to improve regulation and many (63%) also wanted punitive action against violators.[2] Inspite of poor controls, farmers in the middle reaches experienced some increase in the water availability due to works carried out to reduce water wastage in transit.[3] This is quite plausible, because the head reach farmers monopolise the use of water while the tail areas had not received satisfactory water even now. As a result, while the tail end farmers actively participated in the reform process, they were also more frustrated, angry and dissatisfied regarding water availability. This was reflected in the total disinclination to pay their water dues. See the Table 3.1.

See Table 3.2 for WUAs under WD wherein WUAs No. 15-19 at the head did not experience any increase in the area irrigated (colm. 5) as they were already completely irrigated. WUA No. 20 had maximum bridge of ayacut gap, while tail end WUAs No. 21, 22 and 23 had only 25% of ayacut bridged of WUA No. 20 Table 3.3 for D-89 shows highest proportion (68%) of ayacut developed in the WUA at the head reach i.e. Nagnoor I. The last WUA of Chamanpalli did have 77% ayacut increase, but the high figure is explained by the predominance of irrigated

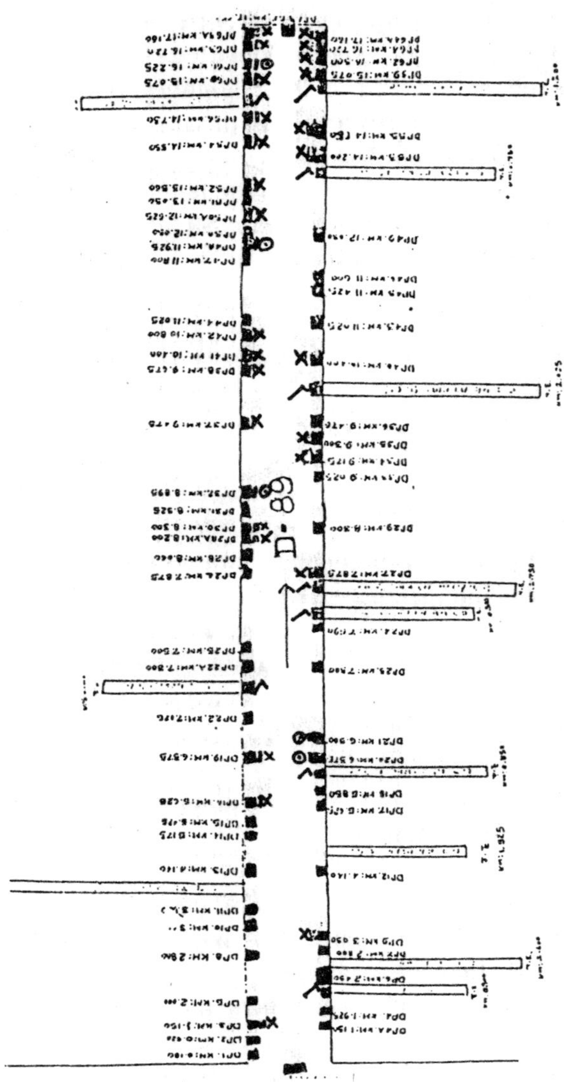

FIG. : 3.1: Kakatiya Main Canal

TABLE 3.1: Farmer Responses in Field Areas under SRSP and NSP

S. No.	Questions asked	Options	Response as %
1.	Elections were	Fair	100
		Unfair	—
2.	Maintenance after PIM was	Same	15
		Worse	—
		Distinct improvement	85
3.	Change in area irrigated after PIM	Yes	27
		No	73
4.	Change in per acre yield of Rice due to PIM	Yes	11
		No	89
5.	Have you been paying water dues as per	Revised rates	15
		Old rates	40
		Not paying	45
6.	Suggestions for controlling water distribution	Installation of shutters	82
		Punitive action*	63
		Miscellaneous	Controls required not only for letting the water in but also for stopping the flow
7.	Whether women should be involved in PIM activities	Yes	19
		No	78
		Miscellaneous	*Yes but not practical * Does not matter whether man or woman – should be committed and sincere
8.	You prefer dealing with	WUA	60
		Department personnel	28
		Indifferent	12

Contd.

TABLE 3.1: *(Contd.)*

S. No.	Questions asked	Options	Response as %
9.	Do you know the name of your WUA president	Yes	54
		No	46
10.	How many General Body (GB) meetings have been held in your WUA	124	
		2-4	5
		More than 4	-
		None	37
		Don't know	34
11.	Were you informed about the GB meetings and did you attend	Informed and attended	9
		Informed but did not attend	23
		Not informed	69

Source: Field data collected from NSP and SRSP areas during 1998-99.

* The demand came forth vociferously from the farmers at the tail end. Members of one of the very active WUA at the tail of WD, were very angry at the failure to get water during Kharif of 1998-99 inspite of taking an active interest in the formation and conduct of WUA activities. The discontent was particularly sharp in view of the head reach farmers getting a second crop of rice while their single ID crops were thirsting for water.

dry crops– which are a second best choice in the area. If increase in wet areas is included, then highest increase has been in the WUA closest to the head. A large part of the increase in ayacut irrigated in the head reaches of D-89 is accompanied by a shift to wet crops in the upper reaches, also reflecting a disproportionately higher access to increased water availability. Thus while the pattern of ayacut increase in the two distributaries may appear to be different, they are explained by the relatively higher appropriation of water by the upstream farmers compared to tail end cultivators. In absolute terms, however, all areas have experienced an increase in area irrigated. This is probably due to better supplies received by distributaries of SRSP that are closer

TABLE 3.2: Statement Showing Gap Ayacut Bridge during 1998-99 Kharif of NSC, O&M Division, Miryalguda (Wazeerabagh Major DC)

Sl.No. From Head to Tail	WUA		Village	Mandal	Developed gap ayacut (acres)
	Number	Name			
1.	15	Chillapuram	Tungapadu	Miryalguda	Nil
2.	16	Venkatadripalem	Tungapadu	"	"
			Venkatadripalem	"	"
			Chintapally	"	"
			Zaptiveerappa gudem	"	"
				"	"
			Borraipalem	"	"
3.	17	Kottagudem	Chintapally	"	"
			Kistapur	"	"
			Guduru	"	"
			Kothagudem	"	"
			Rudraram	"	"
			Dilwarpur	"	"
			Kondrapolu	"	"
			Keshavapuram	"	"
4.	18	Borraipalem	Chintapally	"	"
			Zaptiveerappa-gudem	"	"
				"	"
			Annaram	"	"
			Borraipalem	"	"
			Dilwarpur	Dhamarcharla	
5.	19	Dilwarpur	Annaram	Miryalguda	
			Dilwarpur	Dhamarcharla	"
6.	20	Kallepalle	Tripuraram	Dhamarcharla	638
			Kallepalle	"	267
			Dhamarcharla	"	143
			Narsapur	"	22
			T. V. gudem	"	99

(Contd.)

Table 3.2: *(Contd.)*

Sl.No. From Head to Tail	WUA Number	WUA Name	Village	Mandal	Developed gap ayacut (acres)
			Veerlapalem		32
			Matoor	Tripuraram	544
			Borraipalem	"	193
			Ragadapa	"	146
				Total	**2084**
7.	21	Kondrapolu	Dilwarpur	Dhamarcharla	Nil
			Kondrapolu	"	158
			Dhamarcharla	"	289
				Total	**447**
8.	22	Dhamarcharla	T. V. gudem	Dhamarcharla	Nil
			Kallepalle	"	"
			Irkigudem	"	"
			Wadapalli	"	524
				Total	**524**
9.	23	Keshavapuram	Kondrapolu	Dhamarcharla	Nil
			Keshavapuram	"	521
				Total	**521**

Source: Executive Engineer, NSC, O&M Division, Miryalguda.

to the head of reservoir. At a macro level this increase could be at the expense of tail end distributaries. Therefore, data has to be interpreted with caution *vis-a-vis* its extrapolation.

Rotation

Rotation of supplies among the distributaries in the main canal of SRSP stage 1 has manifested itself in a distinct improvement of supplies to the downstream areas. While the distributaries till about the middle could be supplied water earlier, water was reaching the tail end distributaries for the last two years. However, the distribution below the distributaries has not recorded any

TABLE 3.3: Particulars of WUAs under Distributary No. D-89

Sl.No.	Name of Mandal	No. of WUA	Name of WUA From head to tail	No.of T.C.s	Localised ayacut in acres	Ayacut developed acres during Rabi 1998-99 after formation of WUAs			Total No.of voters (members of general body of WUA)
						Wet	ID	Total	
1.	Karimnagar	1	Nagnoor I	4	1838	390 (21%)*	865 (47%)	1255 (68%)	239
2.	Karimnagar	2	Ellabotharam	5	1151	155 (14%)	460 (40%)	615 (53%)	461
3.	Karimnagar	3	Irrukulla I	5	1346	130 (10%)	550 (41%)	680 (50%)	501
4.	Karimnagar	4	Irrukulla II	5	1490	430 (25%)	370 (25%)	800 (53%)	781
5.	Sultanabad	5	Gollapalli	5	1511	400 (26%)	440 (29%)	840 (55%)	814
6.	Karimnagar	6	Chamanpalli	5	1988	-	1540 (77%)	1540 (77%)	760
				Total	9327	1505	4225	5730	3555

Source: Executive Engineer, LMD, O&M Division, Karimnagar.
* Figures in parenthesis indicate the area developed as a percent of the localised ayacut.
ID — Irrigated dry

corresponding improvement. The tail end areas of the sample distributaries continue to be deprived of their share of water. There was no effective way of prevailing over the head villages even through the mediation of distributary committee. Supplemental irrigation by wells, which were recharged by the surrounding low-lying area, was the mainstay of the tail areas of D-89 distributary. The farmers mentioned having made a few attempts to monitor the water flow from head areas to their village, but were unsuccessful, as the village just upstream of their village intercepted the supplies. Problems such as these dissuaded any payment of water dues for the last more than 10 years. The minor reaching their field, which had been cleared of weeds, bushes etc. at government expense, was full of weeds again. There was no incentive to maintain the channel in the absence of expectation of receiving any water. One time investment in such a situation also amounts to wastage.

Secondly, even if the system of rotation works ideally it has an inbuilt discrimination against the tail enders. Case of Wazeerabagh distributary on NSP-LC illustrates the point. This channel is closed for two days every fifteen days in order to allow water to feed the downstream distributaries. It has a balancing reservoir towards the tail end of the distributary. When the water stops at the head it continues to flow for two to three days towards the end. But since the flow is progressively reduced this is used to fill up the reservoir and water does not reach further. When the distributary again receives the water after two days, it takes three days to fill up and start irrigating the furthest point possible. The gap of irrigation for the tail end areas, therefore, becomes nearly five days. Added to that is the anyway reduced flow due to transit losses. Rotation, therefore, accentuates the uncertainty and irregularity for downstream areas. By proper regulation of water, sought to be ensured through PIM strategy, which entails equal allocation of water on per acre basis, this problem could be overcome by using extra water (which was now being monopolised by head reach farmers) to be used as an effective buffer in the balancing reservoir.

Size Disability

Quite apart from the locational disadvantage there is also the disadvantage based on the size of land holding. Getting water in a lump sum wets a larger area compared to the same water divided into smaller units of land and entering each piece of land separately. This problem was not found to be that acute among the small landholders of the distributaries located at the head reaches of the canal. However, as we go downstream, along the main canal as well along the distributary the locational and land size disability *vis-a-vis* access to water reinforce each other, with its consequences for agricultural productivity and financial returns as discussed below. Taking rice as a representative crop, we notice that while level of per acre yield of rice does not show any correlation with size, its variation (as perceived by the farmers over the preceding years), correlates with size of land holding. Although yield levels attained would be expected to correlate with water availability from an irrigation source, but due to the existence of alternative irrigation sources such as wells, borewells etc., such a correlation was not observed with one source such as canal or tank. No doubt yield is a function of a number of variables and cannot be explained on the basis of proximity to an irrigation source *per se.* Nevertheless, provision of assured irrigation is the critical pre-requisite for the interplay of other factors such as use of fertiliser and pesticides. Lack of irrigation can limit the exploitation of otherwise favourable production environment. Correlation of land size and locational disadvantage with poor economic indicators such as high per acre yield variability and negative per acre per month incomes accruing to small farmers at the tail end without an alternative irrigation source, (as discussed below from a random sample) is significant in this context.

Field Responses

As of now there does not appear to be any change in the ability to *control and regulate* the supply of water. There are technical constraints of controlling the *supply* of water, which are planned to be overcome by installing shutters during the summer closure period of canals. However, there is yet no assurance that these technical artifacts will not meet the fate of their predecessors. Particularly in the light of poor awareness and motivation levels noticed among the head reaches farmers, as discussed below. The issue requires not merely technical solutions, but more importantly, a political will and social mobilisation effort, to effectively ground rules of equitable water allocation by whatever criteria agreed upon. It will be possible to handle the real challenge of equitable water distribution between areas and within areas, only when it is possible to restrict the free and unbridled access of water. The question of witnessing any change in the direction of *redistribution of water* was posed to groups of farmers and the departmental engineers at the field division offices. The near unanimous response from them was in the negative. The field officers were very categorical about their inability to control or restrict water consumption at the head reaches. The problem continued to persist after the reforms and they did not foresee any likelihood of its mitigation as a result of any provisions implied in the reforms. Water intensive cultivation of paddy crop, they felt, had to be discouraged wherever possible, to reduce water demand at the head reaches and enable extensive cultivation with same quantum of water. In certain cases there were technical constraints of switching away from paddy. The seepage from canals along the bank, makes the soil unfit for irrigated dry cultivation. Similarly rice cultivation in the vicinity, results in lateral seepage and increase in moisture content of the surrounding soil, which has a dampening effect on the yield of irrigated dry crops grown there. However, in case where the option of switching away from rice is technically feasible, it is possible to cultivate a higher acreage of irrigated dry crops with the same quantum of water.

Increased Water Availability

No doubt significant quantum of water has been released for additional irrigation due to reduced wastage resulting from the physical works undertaken to repair the channels. See Tables 3.4

and 3.5 for the works done on distributaries in the field areas and the increase in area irrigated as reported by the irrigation department as per evidence discussed earlier. This is manifested as flow of water reaching further downstream, relative to earlier years. (See the second last column in Tables 3.4 & 3.5 for the two distributaries.) Many farmers in the NSP-LC mentioned that water reached the channel at the tail end after 15 years as a direct result of silt clearance. Instances such as these were cited quite frequently during the course of fieldwork. This has also been reported in official statistics as increase in area irrigated as discussed in the preceding chapters. However, it may be noted that this *increase in water availability is due to water saving measures and not due to redistribution of water from head to tail.*

Secondly, there is a quantum jump in the additional water availability as a result of technical works, which facilitate smooth water flow and reduce transmission losses. See Tables 3.4 and 3.5 for the order of estimates of increased flow in the distributaries as a result of works done in the sample areas. But this is a one-time jump. Repairs critical for the flow were the ones undertaken initially e.g. desilting, plugging the leakage points etc. These opportunities are soon saturated. Further works, such as strengthening of embankments or lining of channels contribute more to sustainability of the system and relatively less to increasing the flow. Additional works therefore, are going to be manifested only as incremental water increases. Therefore, further drastic increase in area irrigated is not expected to occur. Since this has clearly not provided satisfactory irrigation to the entire command, there is need to either redefine the command or institute supply control mechanisms effectively or influence water use pattern. The latter two options will necessarily entail a change in the cropping pattern across the length of the distributaries.

Finally, the quality of additional irrigation claimed in official statistics is not clear. It was found that just the reaching of water in the minor was interpreted as increased area irrigated. 104% increase in area irrigated is clearly an over estimation. Possibly this includes the unauthorised irrigated acreage. While areas under command are not receiving their due, areas out of command are

TABLE 3.4: Works done in Canal Areas after PIM Reforms (1998-1999)

2		Works		Total expenditure (in Rs.)	Additional distance of water travelling due to works (kms.)	How much further down is it possible for the water to travel (kms.)
		Sanctioned (in th Rs.)	Completed			
3	**NSP-LC**					
4	DC	3410	All completed	3174	Upto 25 Kms. (5 kms. Extra)	-
5	WUA-15	140	"	112	1	-
6	WUA-16	245	"	107	1	-
7	WUA-17	258	"	245	1.2	-
8	WUA-18	82	"	72	0.5	-
9	WUA-19	87	"	67	0.7	-
10	WUA-20	348	"	346	0.5	-
11	WUA-21	163	"	123	0.7	-
12	WUA-22	173	"	171	1.1	-
13	WUA-23	255	"	239	1.01	-
11	**LMD**					
12	DC	2	2	1,68,900/-	4 Kms. further down	-
13	WUA-1	3	3	54,183/-		-

(Contd.)

TABLE 3.4: *(Contd.)*

2		Works		Total expenditure (in th. Rs.)	Additional distance of water travelling due to works (kms.)	How much further down is it possible for the water to travel (kms.)
		Sanctioned (in th. Rs.)	Completed			
14	WUA-2	2	2	54,640/-		-
15	WUA-3	2	2	39,622/-		-
16	WUA-4	2	2	41,473/-		-
17	WUA-5	2	2	54,197/-		-
18	WUA-6	5	5	97,950/-		-
			Total	3,42,073/-		

Source : Division office of Irrigation Department at Miryalguda and Karimnagar.

TABLE 3.5: Works Done in Canal Areas after PIM Reforms (1999-2000) in WD

2		Works		Total expenditure (in th. Rs.)	Additional distance of water travelling due to works (kms.)	How much further down is it possible for the water to travel (kms.)
		Sanctioned (in th. Rs.)	Completed			
3	**NSP-LC**					
4	DC	3229	All completed	1236	Upto 28 Kms. (3 kms. Extra)	6
5	WUA-15	224	"	86	1	Reached tail end
6	WUA-16	329	"	127	0.5	"
7	WUA-17	563	"	217	1	"
8	WUA-18	144	"	55	0.75	"
9	WUA-19	127	"	49	0.8	"
10	WUA-20	749	"	289	1	Still to reach tail end
11	WUA-21	245	"	95	1	"
12	WUA-22	346	"	134	1.5	"
13	WUA-23	476	"	184	1	"

Source : Division office of Irrigation Department at Miryalguda and Karimnagar.

accessing irrigation, the extent of each is very difficult to estimate. Clearly the inference is not justified by ground realities as noticed during personal visits to the field areas and results in an overestimation of increased water availability. This also raises the very important issue of the criteria underlying the demarcation of irrigation commands. For example, one of the architects of PIM programme in A.P.[4] mentioned that,

"Major irrigation projects in our...country suffer from certain deficiencies particularly in ensuing equity. Some of these are:

(i) Water availability is not correctly assessed. More often it is over assessed to improve the viability of project. Thus, tail end areas suffer as a result, as there is no water available, to be provided to these areas.

(ii) The Command Areas are delineated not entirely on hydraulic basis. I have found that certain which are commendable are left out and certain areas, which are not commendable are included. The classic case is that of the Nagarjuna Sagar Project where a huge extent of land in the upper reaches was excluded whereas uncommendable reaches in the tail end such as in Guntur and Prakasam districts were included. More often non- technical reasons such as political considerations influence delineation of the command areas. This results in (a) clamour for water in areas when water just cannot be conveyed and (b) areas where water is possible to convey and is in fact used, that area is being treated as being under unauthorised or illegal cultivation.

(iii) In order to improve viability, excessive areas are shown as commendable when there are no adequate inflows or storage capabilities in the project to provide irrigation to the notified command areas. This again results in large tracts becoming so called tail end areas.

(iv) The viability of the project is often boosted up by including an irrigated dry crops cropping pattern for the command area, when we fully know that some areas due to their location, soils, etc., are not amenable to cultivation of Irrigated Dry crops. This is noticed under the SRSP.

(v) The cropping pattern prescribed often do not take into account the existing cropping patterns in the areas, preferences of the farmers their land holding patterns, as well as availability of supporting infrastructure such as inputs availability, marketing and processing of the produce area. The absence of such infrastructure discourages farmers to change the cropping patterns and adopt new crops which use lesser quantities of water.

(vi) I am also aware of the fact that in certain projects there are a number of design deficiencies in the canals, outlets etc., which often render full utilisation of the irrigation potential created difficult to achieve. Further in order to

> push water to the non-commendable notified areas, works are taken up to redesign, remodify the irrigation conveyance systems at huge costs (e.g. lift irrigation schemes under the NSP). This results in projects remaining incomplete endlessly with enormous cost overruns. The above reasons essentially create this vexatious problem of ensuring equitable distribution of water particularly between the upper and tail end areas and the consequent and attendant problems that go with it".

See pictures alongside contrasting the head and tail regions at the same time during the same year. More importantly, this points to the need for developing a more representative index for quality of irrigation incorporating indicator of control over water application and certainty or dependability of supply.

Water Wastage

Water wastage in the head reach areas of the canal-irrigated areas was very prominent. Excessive watering of the rice crop in upper reaches of the distributaries was manifested as discharge of underground excess water as a flowing back to the river or drains. This is known as regenerated water.[5] No direct estimation of this wastage was available from the department. But absence of control structures and continuous flow of water preempted a close monitoring of water let into the field. Rice is perceived as a crop that is convenient for cultivation in so far as the cultivator can take it easy once the transplanting is over. All that was required was the submergence of the field the tendency was to always over water as a security rather than take the risk of under watering. Specially as water was easily available at the head and in plenty. Ironically this reverse flow was present in areas where the tail areas were being starved of their legitimate due.

While the subsurface wastage due to over irrigation continues, channel improvement activities have led to significant reduction of wastage due to surface overflows or outflows. An indirect method of estimating the reduction of wastage is to look at the variation of irrigated area per unit of water or what is known as the 'duty' in irrigation parlance. Of course this index has limitations

Head reach areas under Wazeerabagh distributary during a low rainfall year (1999)

Tail end area under the same distributary during a normal rainfall year (1998)

in so far as it does not capture the changes in cropping pattern. If we look at the variation in total area divided by the total water supplied at the head of the distributary over different seasons/ years, then a sharp rise should be evident during the last two years of 1998 and 1999 over the previous years. See Table 3.6 for evidence for WD, based on irrigation department and revenue data. This increase in duty reflects increased efficiency of water use due to reduced wastage as a result of works like silt clearance, construction of drops etc.—all of which facilitate smooth flow of water. The division engineers as increased flow of water in the channels as noted above corroborate this.

The above indicates that there is potential for additional mobilisation of water resources by controlling wastage and increasing area irrigated without affecting the differential and discriminatory use of water by head reach farmers. Schemes to utilize about 20% of the subsurface reverse flow were in operation in the NSP-LC area. These are small lift schemes where water is diverted from drainage streams to irrigate areas further away.

Conclusion

The hypothesis regarding PIM resulting in a greater control over water use and increasing the equity of distribution is not validated from the field investigations. Whatever increase in irrigation has come about, it is the result of reduced wastage in surface flows due to revamping of the supply network of irrigation channels. This has its limits and may be soon saturated as a source of additional irrigation. There is the possibility of installing technical structures for controlling and regulating water supply in the near future. However, a genuine *redistribution* of water although politically challenging holds the ultimate promise of releasing water for downstream farmers. This perception was reflected in the farmers insisting on punitive action for illegal extraction of water. The redistribution is also necessary for ensuring equity in distribution of water in proportion to land cultivated as per the professed criteria of the government. The present system of water

Regenerated water from paddy fields flowing back to river

TABLE 3.6: Irrigated Acreage Per Unit of Water (Duty)
Wazeerabagh Distributary

Year	Area irrigated Total equivalent in wet hectares		Water released in MM^3 (million meter cube)	Duty Colm. 2 or 3/Colm. 4	
	Irrigation dept. data	Revenue data		Irrigation data	Revenue data
1991-92	15010		257.79	58.3	
1992-93	17282		NA	-	
1993-94	15163		278.7	54.41	
1994-95	10503	11517	187.3	56.08	61.49
1995-96	8783	7544	187.3	46.65	40.28
1996-97	12310	10101	241.0	51.08	41.91
1997-98	9296	7829	190.0	48.93	41.21
1998-99	19811	12322	284.0	69.76	43.39

Source: Chief Engineers Office at NSP Hill Colony, Sagar, and computed from data from MROs offices of Miryalguda, Dharamacherla and Tripuravaram and data from division office of irrigation department at Miryalguda, District Nalgonda.

distribution exists by default in the absence of any effective regulatory mechanism resulting in disproportionate withdrawals of water by head reach farmers amounting to a discrimination against the downstream farmers. In addition, there is the likelihood of the new control structures also being tampered with. It is not clear how the reform provisions will prevent this. Secondly, it is extremely unpractical to install control structures and facilities for volumetric supply at all the minor heads and pipe outlets. What then might be the social or community measures to share water equitably according to well-defined and accepted rules is the question, which is *not* being posed.

As noted above, redistribution of water implies equal distribution on per acre basis, as stipulated in the government policy. This is necessary for ensuring equal opportunity for all the landholders to enhance productivity on their lands with consequent income flows. This is imperative from equity considerations as it influences the income and employment opportunities that are possible. It may in addition, lead to higher productivity levels at the macro level. For instance if farmers are given a certain limited ration of water – they are forced to spread it across their cultivable area by growing a combination of wet and irrigated dry crops. Less water will irrigate same area, which may currently be devoted to rice due to uncontrolled access to water. The released quantum will be used to cater to the lands of other farmers on a *pro rata* basis with similar cropping pattern—that is the farmers who were hitherto denied irrigation for their entire area. This will lead to additional productivity on gross area brought under cultivation.

The point is that the head reach farmers make their production decisions with only land as the scarce resource. The proposition being hypothesized is that water too should enter their calculation as a scarce resource for efficient utilisation. Secondly, water constraint at the level of individual producer, will result in extensive use of water, greater land coverage, and higher quantum of agricultural produce in addition to generating more employment. This would be achieved without compromising the economic returns of even the head reach farmer. The macro and micro objectives would complement each other. The above is possible only if water control and regulation rules are instituted effectively. Ensuring equality of water supply (per acre) to all is a desirable objective. Whether this is possible technically or there exist alternative criteria of equitable water distribution are pertinent issues for further research. Cropping pattern can be expected to be different under 'equal' water supply. But whether rice will still be grown, even though on a limited scale, is left for the individual farmers to decide. Warabandi and water pricing are some of the methods of water regulation tried elsewhere. However, their indiscriminate applicability in a different environment cannot be taken for granted. In the appendix we have drawn attention to the limitations of water pricing as a means of water regulation by inducing efficient water use.

NOTES

1. During discussions with field officers, instances of political interference to release water on a priority basis to specific distributaries were often cited as significant pressures which constrain the ability of division office personnel to release water on just and need based criteria.
2. From Tables 4.2, 4.3 & 4.4 for all the field areas, very few water users reported an increase in area irrigated after PIM, even after a good rainfall year. Increase would be expected only in the middle reach farmers. The sample size however, was too small to capture this.
3. It is reflected in the overall data of the WD.
4. Personal communication by Commissioner (CADA) during the years the PIM programme was formulated and initiated.
5. The regenerated flow of the order of 20 to 30 cusecs often compares with that of a minor.

4

PIM, AGRICULTURAL PRODUCTIVITY AND WATER EFFICIENCY

One of the foremost motivations underlying the institution of PIM, was the deplorable state of performance of the irrigation system in AP as discussed above. The irrigated acreage was actually going down under some of the systems. (Jairath, 1999).

This was well acknowledged within the government circles, in particular for its implications for realisation of irrigation potential created.

> "The state of Andhra Pradesh has invested large amounts of its scarce financial resources to create irrigation schemes. The net irrigational potential created thus far 6.4 M ha. Inspite of this large effort, statistics show that only about 4.3 M ha or 67% of the potential created is utilised thus leaving a gap of 2.1 M ha or 33% unutilised. Some of the main reasons for this gap are the *non-compliance of farmers to the designed cropping pattern*, (emphasis added) the poor conditions of the irrigation systems, and the lack of operational plans. In addition to this gap, water distribution within the command areas is often neither reliable nor equitable with large differences in water availability between the head and tail end of the irrigation canals.
>
> "Irrigation and CAD Dept., has attempted to remedy this situation through various measures among which are the rehabilitation of the distribution networks, the introduction of rotational water supply based on structured systems and the promulgation of the AP Irrigation Utilisation and Command Area Development Act, 1984 authorising the creation of Command Area Development Authorities (CAD) and the formation of Pipe Committees. Though some improvements were noted, much of the disorders noted previously continue and none of these initiatives have really proved to be fully *sustainable* (emphasis added). The failure is

> mostly due to a top-down approach to irrigation planning and management without adequate consultation with farmers." (Action Plan, GOAP, 1995).

Without any secular reduction in availability of water, this state of affairs would reflect declining *productivity* of water i.e. output per unit of water. However, computation of output is complex as it depends on the cropping pattern, physical yields and crop prices, which vary at different rates for different crops. A simpler index is area irrigated per unit of water. No doubt, this is also a rough index, given the differential demand of water by different crops. However, abstracting from short-term changes in cropping practices, it can constitute a first level indication of the *efficiency* of water use. The productivity of water can be gauged indirectly from the productivity indices of agricultural production i.e. area irrigated, physical yields of major crops, cropping intensity, changes induced in cropping pattern etc.

It was observed that the yields of major crops such as rice were also below the average for irrigated HYV (Jairath, 1999)[1]. Very often more than necessary water was used for rice cultivation in the head reaches, which resulted in outflows as recharge of drains known as *regenerated* water. There is an overbearing preference for rice cultivation—this has consequent implications for high water consumption and difficulty for switching to another crop at ease. Absence of water regulation and priority of rice cultivation by farmers wherever possible was also the basis of inequity in sharing of water among farmers.

The consequences of PIM for enhancing area irrigated, cropping intensity and physical per acre yields therefore holds considerable significance. Any ensuing changes in the cropping pattern are also of interest in so far as their water consumption and output (per unit of water) reflect a more efficient and productive use of water.

PIM and Irrigated Acreage

Feedback from the Field

That the area under irrigation has shown a marked improvement under some of the projects where PIM has been implemented effectively has been widely claimed by the irrigation department. See Table 4.1 for NSP and SRSP field areas for evidence for ayacut bridged. Field visits to the sample areas also verified that water had in fact reached further downstream in some of the channels where silting, clearing etc. had been undertaken. While this is understandable and plausible, the extent to which this increased flow could contribute to increased irrigation comprising requisite number of wetting i.e. adequate irrigation—is the moot question. For example, on Wazeerabagh distributary while the DC president reported 100% irrigation in the post PIM period, it was found that areas where the water was barely touching were also counted as areas recently irrigated. Secondly, significant chunks of high level areas—declared as non-localised—did not and could not receive irrigation. The argument of their not being authorised or localised does not hold water as they are within the command or should be within the command and be entitled to their share of irrigation as discussed earlier.

More importantly, what is quoted as the increase in area irrigated does not indicate the quality of irrigation in terms of quantum of water available and does not specify the degree of certainty. The *quality* of irrigation accessible to the user is however, crucial for production decisions of the farmers and the eventual profitability level realised. Therefore the reported increase in area irrigated has to be interpreted with caution. It is possible that there has been a qualitative and distinct improvement in the irrigation water availability after the organisation of WUAs and the initiatives undertaken to clean and clear the channels, repair the drops etc. This is reflected in water travelling further downstream as noted above. It is also confirmed from feedback survey conducted by the Department during the various Sadassus of WUA and DC presidents and office bearers. (Feedback, 1998,1999). Repairs such as these were long overdue. However, the *extent* of this additional area is first, overstated and second, it is a one-time increase. There is little likelihood of sustainability of increase at this rate. The percentage increase in area irrigated will be highest during the initial stages, since the original state of maintenance

TABLE 4.1: Yearwise Area Irrigated Wazeerabagh Distributary (NSP) and D-89 Distributary (Karimnagar) (hectares)

Year	KHARIF Total Area Irrig.			RABI Total Area Irrig.		
	Wet	ID	Total	Wet	ID	Total
			WAZEERABAGH DISTRIBUTARY			
1989-90	8541 (72%)*	3361 (28%)	11902	3384 (38%)	5620	9004
-	-	-	-	-	-	-
1996-97	8000	400	8400	200(2%)	9000 (98%)	9200
1997-98	6800 (73%)	2552 (27%)	9352	9000 (82%)	2000 (18%)	11000
1998-99	8900 (83%)	1823 (17%)	10723			
			D-89 DISTRIBUTARY			
1989-90				270	254	524
-	-	-	-	-	-	-
1996-97				1581	3773	5314
1997-98	207 (40%)	342 (60%)	518	1537 (27%)	4244 (73%)	5781
1998-99	1940(55%)	1610 (45%)	3550	22102 (29%)	5330 (71%)	7540

Source: Executive Engineer, M&O division, NSP LC, Myrialguda and Executive Engineer, M&O division, LMD, Karimnagar

*Figures in parenthesis indicate percentage of total area irrigated for that year.

was very poor. The result will therefore, be very marked and distinct. Subsequent improvements are likely to induce incremental increase in irrigated acreage.

While the irrigated acreage cannot be expected to increase indefinitely, the point of initial quantum increase not being sustainable is that most of the increase possible by reducing wastage had taken place and further avenues for increasing area irrigated through channel improvement at the terminal level are limited. No doubt water wastage through outflow of drainage water from paddy fields can be harnessed for further increase in area irrigated or intensity of cultivation. Subsequent to waste reduction—and this by itself may not be able to irrigate the designed command—further ability to meet the water demands of the area left over will depend on water releases due to better regulation and redistribution of water from head to downstream areas. This relates to the issue of adequacy of the designed command as noted above. Are the assumptions of cropping pattern that go into delineating a given command legitimate and reasonable or can they be reviewed to redefine the command fit the area actually being cultivated—even if only for wet crops? The latter approach would rationalise the *status quo* and exclude the tail enders from their right to water. This would amount to legitimising the discrimination faced by them. In addition, by reducing the area within a command, the calculation of cost of irrigation development per acre would rise. As of now this cost is highest for canal irrigation as noted in a later chapter. Such a situation would call for a review of the investment decisions in favour of irrigation by canals compared to other surface and ground water sources of irrigation, which are technically feasible in the area.

A more viable approach would be to explore technologies which entail alternative patterns of water use over not only existing command but possibly beyond that as well. In contrast to the approach above, the command could be redefined to *enlarge* the area sought to be irrigated. The advantages in terms of spreading irrigation benefit over larger area and number of cultivators, along with resulting higher total output, would simultaneously serve the objectives of growth and equity.

Finally, as pointed earlier we have to look at the *source* of this recognised increase in irrigated area in the state of AP—where did this extra quantum of water come from? Was it from a reduction of wastage during transit or from a redistribution of water, which was formerly being appropriated by the upstream farmers or both? There is as yet no evidence from the field visits or from the official records that there has been any redistribution. This is a political sensitive issue and being avoided for understandable reasons. Clearly it is the surplus or the wastage that has been partially mobilised for productive use. And this is no doubt a desirable development. But whether this is sufficient by itself to enable further increase in irrigated acreage is by no means certain. The hunch is that once the scope of the above noted source of area increase is exhausted, further increase will depend on the ability of the government to impose redistribution of water strictly according to the principle of water distribution in proportion to the land cultivated. This is likely to be an unpopular move and has built-in confrontation elements. Conflicting interests of tail—head farmers may not be that easy to resolve. But that is also where the real challenge lies. Particularly, in view of the fact that PIM in AP is a top down programme—with hardly any grass root efforts to mobilise the community. Neither has there been any sensitisation of the users to water as a limited natural resource with multiple uses and entitlements of the entire community to use. There is need for a social discipline in the exploitation of a common property resource such as water since the externalities of its use bear on the entire community. Monopoly by a section of the community, with adverse implications for the others requires to be checked by the government as the largest regulating authority.

Data from the field areas for tank and canal irrigated areas is shown in Tables 4.2, 4.3 and 4.4. While no conclusive evidence emerges in the tank-irrigated areas, the canal-irrigated areas show some increase for the farmers at the middle reaches of WD. The sample however, is too small to capture the overall increase under the distributary. Total data for the distributary is shown in Table 3.2 shows marginal increase for tail WUAs and highest for WUA

#20, as discussed above, which is at the middle reach. This reinforces the argument above i.e. the head continues to have comfortable water, the middle experienced marginal improvement, the tail continues to suffer erratic and low supplies, inspite of water 'touching' the tail end on Wazeerabagh distributary for the first time in the last 15 years. For D-89 maximum increase is at the tail end WUA but only for Irrigated Dry crops. For the wet crops the increase in area is in proportion to the proximity to the source i.e. canal. As noted above for D-89 highest increase of wet irrigated acreage was at the head WUA. (See Table 3.3). In the case of D-89 the use of increased water availability has been used to shift from I to wet crops i.e. to rice cultivation. This is corroborated by data in Table 4.1, where columns 4,5,6 for Rabi 1997 and 1998, show an increase of nearly 600% of total area irrigated where a ratio of 40% wet and 60% Irrigated Dry was reversed to 55% wet and 45% Irrigated Dry—indicating a shift to rice cultivation. For Rabi also there is a mild shift to rice from 27% to 29%. Same trend is evident in NSP. (See Table 4.1) While Kharif wet area shifts from 73% to 83%, for Rabi there is a dramatic shift from 2 to 82%.

Given the unreliability of the irrigation statistics much weight should not be added to absolute numbers. But that there is a shift to wet crops with more water availability with increased water availability during the post-reform period was also confirmed during the field work. In fact, the shift to wet crops underestimates the area increase that is possible with additional water released since water required per acre is higher. Overall, therefore, we notice the fact of increase in area irrigated, which is however, overestimated and a proportional shift to wet crops that is mainly rice in this region.

Field visits to the tail areas bore evidence of insignificant area increase in area irrigated, although the official data indicates significant if not total irrigation[2]. There is a distinct bias to overestimate the area benefited by the reforms. This was corroborated by nil revenue collections from the tail villages of WD-Waddapalli and Irrikigudem (Dharmacherla mandal) for a number of years. No doubt farmers in head and middle reach also

TABLE 4.2: Production Data for NSP Canal Irrigated Area (1998-99)

Distributary	Minor	Land Size	Total Area TA (acres)	NSA	GSA	GSA/ NSA	Rabi Price A/ Rabi@	Av. Yld. Rice Bags	Var. of Yld. of Rice Bags	Yield Var. Avg. Yield of Rice #	Fertilizer per acre # (bags $)	Pesticides per acre # (ltrs)	Output price for Rice Rs.	Other irrig. source well	Water cess paid (Y/N)	Area incrs after PIM	Yld. incrs after PIM
		L	8	8	16	2	87.5%	32	8	25%	4	0.75	500	0	N	N	N
	H	M	4	4	8	2	100%	32	12	38%	4	0.75	400	0	N	N	N
		S	3	3	6	2	100%	32	16	50%	3	0.50	400	0	N	Y	N
		L	7	7	14	2	86%	32	8	25%	4	0.50	500	0	Y	N	N
H	M	M	4	4	8	2	100%	32	14	44%	4	0.00	400	0	N	N	N
		S	1.5	1.5	3	2	100%	32	16	50%	3	0.50	400	0	Y	N	N
		L	8	8	16	2	75%	32	9	28%	4	0.50	450	1	N	N	N
	T	M	5	5	10	2	80%	30	10	33%	4	0.50	450	1	N	N	N
		S	3	3	6	2	67%	32	16	50%	4	0.75	450	0	N	N	N
		L	7	7	14	2	*71%	35	8	23%	4	0.50	500	0	Y	N	N
	H	M	5	5	10	2	*80%	32	10	31%	3	0.50	450	0	N	N	N
		S	4	4	8	2	*75%	26	10	38%	4	0.50	500	0	Y	Y	N
		L	9	9	18	2	*78%	35	8	23%	4	0.75	500	0	Y	N	N
M	M	M	6	6	12	2	*67%	32	9	28%	4	0.50	450	0	Y	Y	N
		S	1.5	1.5	3	2	*75%	25	16	64%	4	3.00	400	0	N	N	N
		L	8	8	16	2	*75%	36	10	28%	3	0.75	575	0	Y	N	N
	T	M	5	5	10	2	*80%	30	9	30%	4	0.50	550	0	Y	N	N
		S	2	2	4	2	*50%	28	16	57%	4	0.75	540	0	N	N	N

(Contd.)

TABLE 4.2: *(Contd.)*

Dis-tri buta-ry	Mi-nor	Land Size	Total Area TA (acres)	NSA	GSA	GSA/ NSA	Rabi Price A/ Rabi@	Av. Yld. Rice Bags	Var. of Yld. of Rice Bags	Yield Var. Avg. Yield of Rice #	Fer-tili-zer per acre # (bags $)	Pesti-cides per acre # (ltrs)	Out-put price for Rice Rs.	Other irrig. source well	Water cess paid (Y/N)	Area incrs after PIM	Yld. incrs after PIM
		L	7	7	14	2	0%	33	8	24%	4	0.50	650	1	N	N	N
	H	M	6	6	12	2	0%	32	10	32%	4	0.75	550	1	N	N	N
		S	3	3	6	2	0%	30	14	47%	3	0.50	540	1	N	N	N
		L	10	10	20	2	0%	30	9	30%	4	0.75	600	1	N	N	N
T	M	M	5	5	10	2	0%	0	0					0	N	N	
		S	2	2	4	2	0%	28	16	57%	5	0.75	550	1	N	N	N
		L	18	18	36	1.4	*44%	35	5	14%	5	0.75	650	1	N	N	N
	T	M	6	6	12	1.7	*44%	30	5	17%	5	0.75	540	1	N	N	N
		S	3	3	6	1.7	*33%	32	16	50%	5	0.75	540	0	N	N	N

Source . Data Collected during field work in the sample areas

* Low lying areas close to the Krishna River bed which has a good potential for charging open wells

@ Areas devoted to rice as as a percentage of total area cultivated during Rabi

$ These are standard bags bought by the farmers and each weighs 150kgs

Calculated from the preceding column divided by the average yield.

TABLE 4.3: Production Data for SRSP Canal Irrigated Area (1998-99)

Distributary	Minor	Land Size	Total Area TA (acres)	NSA	GSA	GSA/ NSA	Rabi Price A/ Rabi@	Av. Yld. Rice Bags	Var. of Yld. of Rice Bags	Yield Var. Avg. Yield of Rice #	Fertilizer per acre # (bags $)	Pesticides per acre # (ltrs)	Output price for Rice Rs.	Other irrig. source well	Water cess paid (Y/N)	Area incrs after PIM	Yld. incrs after PIM
		L	10	10	14	1.4	40%	35	10	29%	3	6	450	Y	N	N	N
	H	M	6	6	12	2.0	67%	30	10	33%	5	2	450	N	N	N	N
		S	1	1	2	2.0	100%	30	15	50%	3	2	430	N	N	N	N
		L	15	15	30	2.0	53%	38	3	8%	6	0.5	430	Y	N	N	N
H	M	M	6	6	12	2.0	50%	38	15	39%	3	2	450	N	N	N	N
		S	2	2	4	2.0	50%	40	20	50%	3	1	500	N	Y	N	N
		L	6	6	12	2.0	67%	35	10	29%	4	2	500	Y	N	N	N
	T	M	6	6	9	1.5	50%	35	15	43%	6	3	450	N	N	N	N
		S	1	1	2	2.0	100%	32	20	63%	5	2	480	N	N	N	N
		L	20	20	35	1.8	40%	35	5	14%	5	2	450	Y	N	N	N
	H	M	4	4	8	2.0	100%	30	15	50%	4	2	450	Y	N	N	N
		S	2	2	4	2.0	50%	30	2	7%	4	2	450	Y	N	N	N
		L	16	16	32	2.0	50%	30	5	17%	4	6	450	Y	N	N	N
M	M	M	5	5	10	2.0	100%	32	8	25%	5	6	450	Y	N	N	N
		S	1.5	1.5	3	2.0	100%	32	12	38%	5	6	450	Y	N	N	N
		L	7	7	12	1.7	43%	30	10	33%	4	6	450	Y	N	N	N
	T	M	4	4	8	2.0	75%	35	15	43%	5	6	450	Y	N	N	N
		S	2	2	4	2.0	100%	30	15	50%	5	2	450	Y	N	N	N

(Contd.)

TABLE 4.3: *(Contd.)*

Dis-tri buta-ry	Mi-nor	Land Size	Total Area TA (acres)	NSA	GSA	GSA/ NSA	Rabi Price A/ Rabi@	Av. Yld. Rice Bags	Var. of Yld. of Rice Bags	Yield Var. Avg. Yield of Rice #	Fer-tili-zer per acre # (bags $)	Pesti-cides per acre # (ltrs)	Out-put price for Rice Rs.	Other irrig. source well	Water cess paid (Y/N)	Area incrs after PIM	Yld. incrs after PIM
		L	6	6	11	1.8	17%	30	10	33%	3	2	500	N	N	N	N
	H	M	5	5	10	2.0	0%	20	5	25%	3	0.5	525	N	N	N	N
		S	1	1	2	2.0	0%	0	0	0%	0	0	0	N	N	N	N
		L	6	6	10	1.7	25%	25	8	32%	3	2	450	N	N	N	N
T	M	M	4	4	8	2.0	0%	0	0	0%	0	0	0	N	N	N	N
		S	3	3	6	2.0	0%	0	0	0%	0	0	0	N	N	N	N
		L	7	7	13	1.9	14%	30	10	33%	4	0.5	500	N	N	N	N
	T	M	4	4	8	2.0	25%	30	15	50%	4	2	430	N	N	N	N
	S	1	1	2	2.0	0%	0	0	0%	0	0	0	N	N	N	N	

TABLE 4.4: Production Data for Tanks (Nos. 1, 2, 3, 4 and 5)

Tank No.	Loc-ation	Land Size	Total Area TA (acres)	NSA	GSA	GSA/NSA	Rabi Price A/ Rabi@	Av. Yld. Rice Bags	Var. of Yld. of Rice Bags	Yield Var. Avg. Yield of Rice #	Fer-tili-zer per acre # (bags $)	Pesti-cides per acre # (ltrs)	Out-put price for Rice Rs.	Other irrig. source well	Water cess paid (Y/N)	Area incrs after PIM	Yld. incrs after PIM
		L	8	8	12	1.5	38.0%	25	6	24%	4	1	500	1	Y	N	N
	H	M	6	6	10	1.7	0%	25	5	20%	4	2	500	1	Y	N	N
		S	3	3	5	1.7	33%	25	10	40%	4	2	470	0	Y	N	N
		L	10	10	14	1.4	30%	24	5	21%	3	1.5	480	1	Y	N	N
1	M	M	5	5	9	1.8	40%	26	6	23%	4	2	450	0	N	N	N
		S	2	2	2	1	4%	25	10	40%	4	1	450	1	Y	N	N
		L	8	8	12	1.5	38%	22	10	45%	4	1	450	1	N	N	N
	T	M	4	4	6	1.5	14%	24	10	42%	3	2	450	1	N	N	N
		S	2	2	2	1	0%	25	15	60%	4	2	500	0	N	N	N
		L	9	9	14	1.6	33%	24	8	33%	4	2	480	1	Y	N	N
	H	M	6	6	10	1.7	33%	25	16	64%	4	2	450	1	N	N	N
		S	0.5	0.5	1	2	100%	27	15	56%	4	2	450	0	Y	N	N
		L	8	8	14	1.8	25%	22	6	27%	3	1	480	1	Y	N	N
2	M	M	6	6	10	1.7	33%	25	8	32%	3	1	480	1	N	N	N
		S	1	1	2	2	100%	24	10	42%	4	2	425	0	N	N	N
		L	7	7	10	1.4	33%	25	5	20%	4	2	450	1	Y	N	N
	T	M	3	3	6	2	100%	25	9	36%	4	1.5	450	0	N	N	N
		S	2.5	2.5	5	2	40%	21	8	38%	4	1	430	0	N	N	N

(Contd.)

TABLE 4.4: *(Contd.)*

Tank No.	Location	Land Size	Total Area TA (acres)	NSA	GSA	GSA/ NSA	Rabi Price A/ Rabi@	Av. Yld. Rice Bags	Var. of Yld. of Rice Bags	Yield Var. Avg. Yield of Rice #	Fertilizer per acre # (bags $)	Pesticides per acre # (ltrs)	Output price for Rice Rs.	Other irrig. source well	Water cess paid (Y/N)	Area incrs after PIM	Yld. incrs after PIM
		L	7	7	12	1.7	29%	22	5	23%	4	1	450	0	N	N	N
	H	M	4	4	7	1.8	25%	24	8	33%	3	2	470	0	N	N	N
		S	2	2	2	1	100%	20	9	45%	3	1.5	450	1	N	N	N
		L	8	8	12	1.8	38.0	25	8	32%	4	2	480	1	Y	N	N
3	M	M	6	6	10	1.7	33%	24	10	42%	3	2	450	0	Y	N	N
		S	3	3	5	1.7	0%	26	15	58%	3	2	430	1	N	N	N
		L	5	5	10	2	0%	25	8	32%	4	2	450	1	N	N	N
	T	M	4	4	7	1.8	0%	24	6	25%	4	2	450	1	Y	N	N
		S	3	3	5	1.7	0%	21	10	48%	4	1	450	0	N	N	N
		L	7	7	12	1.7	38%	24	5	21%	3	2	550	0	Y	N	N
	H	M	5	5	7	1.4	0%	25	8	32%	4	1	500	1	N	Y	N
		S	3	3	5	1.7	33%	26	10	38%	3	1	450	1	N	N	N
		L	8	8	14	1.8	30%	24	6	25%	4	2	450	1	Y	N	N
4	M	M	4	4	6	1.5	40%	25	7	28%	3	1	450	1	N	N	N
		S	2	2	2	1.0	0%	25	10	40%	3	2	430	0	Y	N	N
		L	6	6	10	1.7	38%	22	10	45%	4	2	450	1	Y	N	N

TABLE 4.4: *(Contd.)*

Tank No.	Location	Land Size	Total Area TA (acres)	NSA	GSA	GSA/NSA	Rabi Price A/Rabi@	Av. Yld. Rice Bags	Var. of Yld. of Rice Bags	Yield Var. Avg. Yield of Rice #	Fertilizer per acre # (bags $)	Pesticides per acre # (ltrs).	Output price for Rice Rs.	Other irrig. source well	Water cess paid (Y/N)	Area incrs after PIM	Yld. incrs after PIM
	T	M	4	4	6	1.5	25%	25	8	32%	4	1	480	0	N	N	N
		S	1	1	1	1.0	0%	0	0	0%	4	2	450	0	Y	N	N
		L	6	6	9	1.5	33%	24	8	33%	3	1	480	1	N	N	N
	H	M	5	5	4	0.8	33%	22	16	73%	4	2	450	0	N	N	N
		S	2	2	3	1.5	0%	0	0	0%	4	1	420	0	Y	N	N
		L	7	7	10	1.4	25%	25	6	25%	4	2	450	1	Y	N	N
5	M	M	4	4	3	0.8	33%	24	7	29%	4	1	480	1	Y	N	N
		S	2	2	2	1.0	50%	22	10	45%	3	1	430	0	N	N	N
		L	7	7	10	1.4	33%	25	5	20%	4	2	450	1	N	N	N
	T	M	4	4	6	1.5	30%	25	8	32%	3	2	430	1	N	N	N
		S	3	3	5	1.7	33%	21	9	43%	3	1	420	0	N	N	N

defaulted on their payments. But tail end farmers refused to pay the water charges as a right and not due to paucity of funds that was cited as a reason by those who did not pay inspite of getting sufficient water.

PIM and Yields

The next issue is the impact of PIM on the yields of the major crops. A lot has been published on water in relation to crop growth and attempts to understand crop responses to water through crop growth modelling under different growing conditions and input combination. It has been pointed that "the upper limit of crop production is set by climatic conditions and the genetic potential of the crop. The extent to which this limit can be reached will always depend on how finely the engineering aspects of water supply are in tune with the biological needs of water in crop production. Therefore, efficient use of water in crop production can only be attained when planning design and operation of water supply and distribution is geared towards meeting in quantity and time including periods of water shortage, the crop needs required for optimum growth and high yields" (Doorenboss and Kassan, 1997:2). Given the yield response curves to water application it is possible that total output reductions due to reduced water application vary for different crop combinations on a farm. A higher proportion of water insensitive crops in the annual production package will reduce the fluctuations in the total out put due to variations in available irrigation water, which may be inevitable due to climatic factors. PIM is expected to influence total productivity and per acre yields by enhancing controlled water application as well as inducing changes in crop combination due to water rationing.

Increase in per acre yields, especially of rice is an issue that is occasionally touched upon while highlighting the achievements of PIM, although not with equal force. It is very difficult to comment on the validity of the hypothesis that crop yields have increased as a result of PIM—in fact, this claim is not forcefully made even in the case of Irrigation Management Transfer (IMT) in Mexico, which is recognised as a success story of PIM. Impact assessment study for the Alto Rio Lerma region states that there has been no impact of the irrigation transfer programme in the area on economic and agricultural productivity, including physical yields and even area irrigated. (Johnson. *et al,* 1997). Yield changes are a function of a complex set of variables including natural-climatic, technological and timeliness of input availability and cannot be obviously related to reforms in the irrigation sector *per se.* Secondly, it is probably too early to comment either way on the direction of impact on the physical yields. Field data from both canal and tank irrigated areas do not indicate any trend of increase in the yield of rice over the last two years inspite of the potential to increase, given the average yield of about 2500 kgs. per acre.

An interesting response during field visits from canal commands points to lower rice yields in head reach areas which are right next to the canals, compared to other areas which have surplus water. This points to diminishing returns to water application and ironically low water productivity *inspite of and because of surplus water*—in the absence of adequate control structures. However data collected does not bring out this point. Since this was quoted frequently and independently during discussions with farmers and division engineers, there is need to explain the anomaly. Especially since average yield in the head reach areas is marginally higher compared to the downstream yields for SRSP and NSP areas. It is possible that seepage in fields close to canals (upto half a kilometer) did depress the yields by about 5 bags per acre, other things being same. Beyond this stretch however, the impact of plenty of water, which is drained out, shows up in higher yields in lands beyond the seepage belt. It is the locking in of the water along canal banks that is responsible for depressing the yields in that region.

Significant correlation of variation of yields of rice with size of land holding was observed, indicating the precarious position of the small landowner. These variations would be expected to get worse as one moves away from the irrigation source. However, field observations do not bear this out. This could be explained by access to alternative sources. It may be noted that rice can only be grown in the downstream areas on the condition of access to wells/borewells/tanks or possibly in the low lying areas close to the natural drainage such as a river bed, as in the case of some areas of the tail end villages under D-89. The expected trend therefore partially gets neutralised. Use of fertiliser and pesticides are other critical determinants of yield. However, no correlation of per acre use of these inputs was observed with land size and location relative to the irrigation source. Farmers mentioned that use of pesticide often increase the biomass of the output without increasing the seed (i.e. the yield of the grain).

Another indicator of production decision determined by irrigation was the area devoted to rice during Rabi season as it is entirely irrigation dependent cultivation, unlike the rice cultivation during Kharif, in which case expectation of rainfall plays an important role. Although no overall pattern correlating proportion of Rabi Rice cultivation with land size and location was observed from the field data, it was noticed that tail end farmers without wells were unable to cultivate rice during Rabi, which was the sought after crop. This could mean considerable hardship for the small farmers, as they were dependent on rice for their food security. Small size sometimes becomes a constraint even in the head reaches as was illustrated by the case of a farmer with 1.5 acres of land at the head of a tank. This cultivator could not cultivate rice on his land during Rabi because of overall water scarcity of water in the tank, which was demanded by the larger landlords downstream. Neither could he grow irrigated dry crops as seepage from the tank caused high moisture content in the soil that adversely affected the yield of irrigated dry crops He, therefore, left his land fallow. Later, we note how some of the small cultivators have extremely precarious economic existence, operating at bare survival, and often even below that, following from the nature of their access to the irrigation source. This underscores the need for equitable distribution of water. How far PIM has succeeded in redressing this imbalance is the pertinent question.

While the average yield difference in Myralgudda between area affected by canal seepage and that beyond the seepage zone was 3 to 4 bags (1 bag = 70 kgs.) per acre, in Karimnagar area it was 5-10 bags per acre. This area is typically laden with high moisture, thereby being unfit for any other crop besides rice. Being close to the water source ironically, it is also the most heavily watered area. The common explanation for this anomaly in the field appears to be the absence of control structures and/ or inability to conduct controlled water application. Over watering at these reaches is also reflected in the voluminous flow of recharged water that gets drained out as a reverse flow to the river as noted above.

The more important issue regarding irrigation impact on yield was its stabilising role. Better management of the system would contribute to greater stability by ensuring timely and predictable supplies. Although it is not possible to overcome the fluctuations in natural climatic factors, controlled irrigation can often mitigate the adversity. However, no such impact was in evidence. It is also a little too early for such impact to become visible. Taking paddy as a representative crop for the field areas, it was found that fluctuations in yield of paddy were pronounced among the smaller holders towards the tail end areas under both the canal commands. See Figs. 4.1 and 4.2. Equity implications of this reinforce need to redress the tail head discrimination—which is also a stated objective of the irrigation reforms.

PIM and Cropping Pattern and Intensity

The only shift in the cropping pattern induced by the reforms is to reinforce the cultivation of wet crops e.g. rice as discussed above. The farmers are inclined to shift to rice wherever possible. The interesting question is that this is justified by the lack of any feasible alternative—with comparable ease of cultivation and economic returns. When questioned about the readiness to shift given a feasible alternative the response was positive.[3] Another argument put forward by the farmers is that the soil gets addicted to rice and it is not possible to switch over to irrigated dry crops casually during a period of water scarcity. We have noted above that this is a conditional constraint. That it is a food crop does

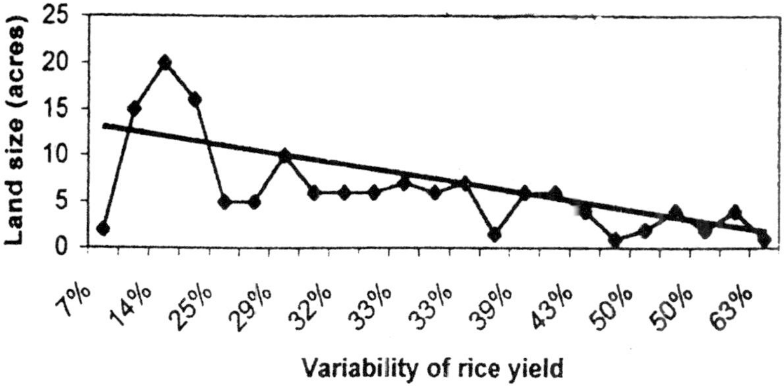

FIG. 4.1: Land Size and Yield Variability (SRSP Canal 1998-99)

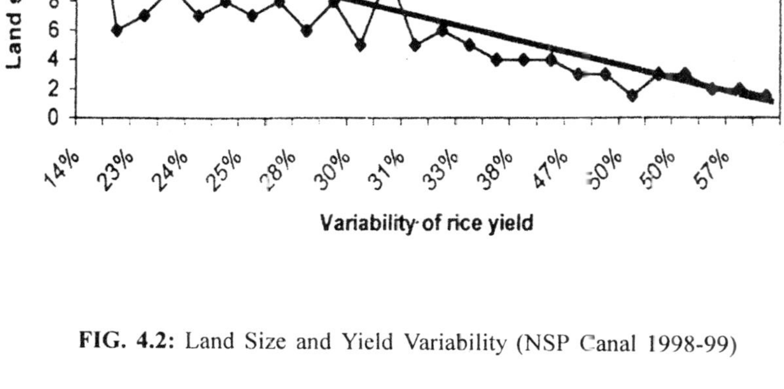

FIG. 4.2: Land Size and Yield Variability (NSP Canal 1998-99)

not explain its being produced as a cash crop as well. While these arguments may be reasonable under some specific conditions—they are not infallible. What is more definitely constraining is the externality of rice cultivation in one field for the neighbouring fields, especially if they are downstream of the rice field. The excessive watering required for rice percolates underground and the seepage may extend laterally. This prevents the viable cultivation of irrigated dry crops in the area. Independent decisions taken by cultivators can limit the choices open to the others in the vicinity is an immediate sense. Feasibility of irrigated dry crops is thereby constrained due to this factor. Some regulation of the cropping pattern by the overall governing authority is required or interventions to promote the cultivation of less water intensive crops.

The proposition above, it may be noted, is not to be confused with what is known as *'localisation'* in irrigation parlance, which refers to a strict prescription of cropping pattern on the cultivators' lands within the irrigation commands. While the concept has been used in irrigation planning since the British days, it has seldom been implemented successful.[4] What is being hypothesised is that the interventions should be targeted at the socio-economic-techno environment of the water user in order to influence his choice of crops in favour of lower water consumption. It is not a compulsive directive of dos and don'ts of land use. That farmer's choice of crops is the net outcome of multiple options and constraints he faces in his immediate environment e.g. climatic factors, personal preferences, price structures, marketing facilities of outputs and inputs, technical feasibility, timeliness of input availability etc. is well acknowledged. To evolve a comprehensive package that stimulates the adoption of extensive water and land-use pattern it is argued should comprise a prominent area of further research.[5] This will enable a possible shift in the *voluntary* decisions of the cultivator. The focus has to be on making the *desired choice attractive to the individual producer.* That is where the challenge lies. The packages could emerge out of joint consultation between the experts and farmers, through pilot experiments, periodic feedback and follow-up, open and public discussions etc. There is certainly a danger in trying out this process in isolation from the farming community. In short, the process of evolving these strategies should also be participatory—in tune with the spirit of the entire programme.

What the above does point to is the need to explore technical alternatives to rice cultivation that can be transferred to the field under actual conditions prevalent in the area. *Transfer of technology* from the lab to the field through practical demonstration along with an active awareness campaign is required. Conscious effort is required to wean farmers away from rice cultivation—which can facilitate equitable water distribution by demonstrating the viability of low water consumption cropping pattern. The latter has to be made attractive to the head reach farmers, atleast beyond the seepage zone, in order for the government to tackle the issue of unpopularity of any measure which aims at reduced water allocation to those who are accustomed to unrestricted supplies (and who could constitute a strong lobby). Mere appeals to their sense of justice are unlikely to motivate them to relinquish their favourable hold. The anticipated resistance by a section of the farmers will also be a disincentive for the political party in power to press hard for the redistributive reforms.

The cropping intensity changes are likely to be witnessed with increase in irrigated area—and to that extent only. As of now, most of the irrigated areas under canal head and middle reaches are double cropped, except the ones under annual crops. Tail end areas without wells have lower CI. Evidence of two tail end villages on WD show the cultivation of only single rain fed crop as there are no wells, tanks, or any other supplemental irrigation scheme in the area. However, if the cropping pattern changes, the cropping intensity will change in proportion as the crops are less water consumptive and, therefore, cover a greater area. No definite clues or trends were noticed from the field data or the secondary data with regard to cropping intensity changes across projects. Concentration of low CIs in the downstream areas under canal irrigation can partly be explained by annual crops such as turmeric, cotton etc. In tail areas under WD land was often left fallow during Rabi—which did not have the benefit of low-lying areas.

This was corroborated by the data collected through secondary sources for the village as a whole. CI under tanks was lower than that under canals. Wherever possible, it was supplemented by well irrigation. Low water availability in tanks was attributed to excessive silt accumulation apart from low rainfall in the catchment area. Some of these tanks are more than 70 years old and given the average life of a tank as 50 years, the tanks had far outlived their lives. Silting had choked them only in the recent years. Some mechanism of periodic silt clearance must have been in operation earlier and/or the rate of silt accumulation must have been slower due to vegetation in the upper catchment areas. In this context, the local farmers mentioned that silt was often used as an important fertiliser and farmers would carry cartloads to their fields. Maintenance of bullocks for carts had become increasingly difficult due to reduction of grazing grounds. In addition, there was the more convenient (even though more expensive) option of buying chemical fertilisers in the market. As a result the above practice was discontinued contributing to silt accumulation. The WUAs primary demand in this region was to either demand finances for silt clearance or the construction of new tanks. On the whole, water availability was found to be less dependable—both due to reduced storage capacity as well as low and erratic rainfall. The latter could be partially neutralised by replenishment through canals. Limited area under canals and lower CI further underscores the need to use water for extensive cultivation to benefit entire area. *Water shortage is artificially created when limited water resources are monopolised by water guzzling crops such as rice.*

NOTES

1. This was pointed out recently by the state Governor during a public lecture. Productivity of rice was only 2494 Kgs. per hectare, which is far below that of Punjab, Haryana and Tamil Nadu. (DC, 1999).
2. The DC president of one of the distributaries proudly boasted of 100% irrigation during our discussions with him just after our field visit to that very area, which comprised barren tracts of land obviously visible which had not been cultivated for quite a few years.

3. It is popularly known as a lazy man's crop in the area.
4. See Mollinga (1999) for a comprehensive discussion of the genesis of the concept and experience with implementation. See also Jurriens and Landstra (1989) for analysis of poor experience with localisation in case of Tugabhadra Scheme in Karnataka
5. "..... *a farmer's decision to grow any food crop is based on a number of factors namely:*
Nature and extent of his/her land holding; Need for food security for the family in view of small size of small holding and lack of employment opportunity to earn non farm incomes; Viability of growing commercial crops or even irrigated dry *crops due to high risk and high investment needs*... In an ideal situation every farmer (who is an entrepreneur) would like to grow such crops, which need the least investment, which evolve the least risk and which give high returns. If one analyses his/her decision making, based on risk, investment and return criteria, cultivation of commercial crops, irrigated dry crops require high levels of investments, higher levels of risks with fluctuating and uncertain returns. A small farmer or a marginal farmer with a very smallholding and a large family prefers to grow rice, which is a staple diet because rice gets reasonable good returns once irrigation is assured. In the case of commercial crops such as cotton, tobacco, chilies, oil seeds, etc., while the returns could be very high yet they are full of risk and uncertainty particularly regarding good quality inputs, high cost on crop management and fluctuating prices for the produce. Therefore, attempts to change the cultivation practices can only succeed if the mechanisms to reduce the risks and investment costs are put in place or minimum returns are assured. Co-operatives and commercial banks have not been able to respond to the task of providing adequate credit to farmers. Co-operatives have also failed to provide marketing support to the farmers. There is need therefore to set up adequate mechanisms to help farmers in decision-making particularly regarding the types of crops to be grown during a particular crop season. Farmers need to have access to market information on the prevailing market prices, they must be exposed to trends in markets and fluctuations in prices, they must have access to value addition to their crops so that the returns can be high, so that they can take well informed judgments on cropping patterns and cultivation practices....." (Commissioner CADA, personal communication).

5

PIM AND FINANCIAL RETURNS

Backdrop

Financial inefficiency experienced typically with most irrigation projects, was another major motivation for the rethinking which led to the organisational reforms in the irrigation sector. It is a well-acknowledged fact, that low financial efficiency and poor financial returns at various levels characterised most irrigation systems projects, especially the large scale ones. First, inefficiencies are noted at the level of creation of irrigation potential. Second, at the level of M&O there is the problem of *insufficiency* of funds as well as *inefficiency* of the utilisation of whatever financial resources that are available. While more than 70% of these resources are spent on administrative expenses known as work charged establishment costs—comprising salaries, infrastructure etc., there is little left for actual execution of the works. Added to that is the poor *quality* of works done with financial implications for repeated maintenance and greater financial requirement. Finally, there is the whole issue of *poor collection* of irrigation revenues as water cess from the users. It is well known that the recovery rates are very poor (see Table 5.1). Department sources have noted that until the 1950s irrigation development used to be financially profitable. Revenues from water charges levied on beneficiary farmers were larger than government expenditures on operation and maintenance and imputed interest on initial investment. Over time however this situation has eroded. The difference from current revenues from major and medium irrigation

TABLE 5.1: Statement showing Year-wise Water Charges collected from Myralgudda Mandal at the Head of NSP LC

Year	Balance Arrears Due as a % of Total Arrears	Amount Collected as a % of Total Settled Demand for the year
1983-84	98	37
1984-85	98	35
1985-86	73	68
1986-87	97	51
1987-88	93	49
1988-89	92	47
1989-90	88	43
1990-91	92	34
1991-92	94	67
1992-93	92	71
1993-94	90	93
1994-95	97	65
1995-96	93	89
1996-97	84	36
1997-98	93	19

Source: Mandal Revenue Office, Miryalguda, District Nalgonda.

projects and non-plan recurring expenditure on these projects has exceeded Rs. 115 crore in 1995-96. (See Table 5.2)

The meagre revenue receipts were responsible for slow development of irrigation potential and poor maintenance. The resource crunch was accentuated by the rise in per hectare cost of new investments. The cost of providing canal irrigation at 1996 prices is estimated at Rs. 50,000 per acre. Accounting for interest on this investment, the annual per acre cost works out to be Rs. 8150. The capital investment cost per acre is as follows (Irrigation Sector—a factual note, 1996, GOAP):

1. Major Projects Rs. 50,000

TABLE 5.2: Revenues from and Expenditure on Major and Medium Projects

(Rs. Crores)

S. No.	Description	1992-93	1993-94	1994-95	1995-96
1.	Revenues	20.44	21.84	25.11	19.06
2.	Non-plan expenditure (Excluding interest borrowing)	139.30	150.70	138.28	133.20
3.	Plan expenditure	579.14	826.06	778.31	648.93
4.	Revenue as % of non-plan expend.	14.67	14.49	18.15	14.31
5.	Expenditure on staff (Plan non plan)	152.16	153.29	181.48	193.99
6.	Revenue as % of staff expenditure	13.43	14.24	13.83	9.82

Source: Irrigation Sector–a factual note, 1996, GOAP.

2.	Medium Projects	Rs. 40,000
3.	Minor Projects	Rs. 35,000

Pre-reform estimates of funds requirement for maintenance of canals, dams and other structures of major and medium projects is worked out at Rs. 120 per acre. As against this the water charges were fixed at Rs..40 to Rs. 60 per acre for different crops. (See Table 5.3 below). These costs did not include establishment and capital cost of the projects. Receipts of revenue from water rates were far below the recurrent expenditure incurred on maintenance and operation of irrigation schemes. As noted by the department, the above criteria of charging fees were barely sufficient to pay for the salaries of the work charged establishment, let alone the capital costs. (Factual Note: 1996)

"The present water rates do not even cover the M&O expenses, let alone yield a return on huge investments made. On the basis of cumulative investments of Rs. 5250 crore made in irrigation

TABLE 5.3: Application of New Water Charges

Sl. No.	Nature of crop	Rates of water cess per acre in respect of Water sources under			
		Category I		Category II	
		Pre-revised#	Revised*	Pre-revised #	Revised*
1.	First or single wet crop	60-00	200-00	40-00	100-00
2.	Second and third wet crop	60-00	150-00	40-00	100-00
3.	First crop irrigated dry	40-00	100-00	20-00	60-00
4.	Second and third crop irrigated dry	40-00	100-00	20-00	60-00
5.	Dufassal crop in fasli year	120-00	350-00	80-00	350-00
6.	Aquaculture per year	0	500-00	0	500-00

Source: Reforming the Irrigation Sector for Sustainable Management and Development, Policy Statement, 13 Nov. 1997.
w.e.f. from 1-7-1989 (pre-revised)
* w.e.f. from 1-7-1996 (revised)

projects till the end of 1995-96 and assuming an interest rate of 8.7% on government borrowing and 1% depreciation on these investments, plus actual O&M expenses, the cost per acre of canal irrigation to government works out to be Rs. 1094. This is in sharp contrast to the water rate of Rs. 40 to Rs. 60 per acre paid by the farmers". (Factual Note, 1996 : 6).

Water Rates—Fixation and Collection

Raising the fees by itself is not sufficient to increase irrigation revenues. We have discussed elsewhere (See Appendix) the limitation of water pricing as a lever for inducing efficient water use. In fact, there has been a steady increase in the official water rates. (See Table 5.3). The critical question is the *extent of compliance* with these rates. Evidence from the field, points to large variation in the payment pattern (See Tables 4.2, 4.3 and 4.4) Defaulting on payments of irrigation fees consistently by tail enders from the field sample, was rooted in their poor access to irrigation from the main source. As noted above, there was a categorical and explicit refusal to pay on their part till the irrigation service was improved.

Fee collection at the tail end continued to be marginal even after the reforms. Thus, claims of providing assured irrigation to the tail areas are not tenable. Even farmers in the head reach areas, which have been getting good water consistently, appear to have defaulted on their payments. The evidence from Myralgudda mandal, which includes villages at the head of WD, shows a maximum of 64% (of the total demand) collections during Rabi season of 1998-99 only. The collections during Kharif were nil. The percent of total demand collected for the year works out to barely 10%. And this is the case in the heart of 'rice bowl' of the country!

Looking at the accumulated picture of collections and balances due, we find that the arrears amount to more than 2.3 crores against most recent collections of less than 45 lacs i.e. more than 80% of water cess is due as of date from this mandal alone in 1999 (Table 5.4). The farmers from this region certainly cannot claim to be suffering from water scarcity. Water rates as pointed above have been revised upwards. Data from MRO's office for the Myralgudda division, on the water charges collected do indicate marginal increase in the absolute quantum of revenue collections. But when this is compared with the revenue expected as per the demands (see Table 5.1 for amounts collected as a proportion of demand and percentage of arrears due) the amount collected at higher rate corresponds to smaller proportion of area cultivated or fewer persons paying their dues. Added to this are the collections made but not deposited. Disaggregated data is required to come to a firm conclusion. It is not clear therefore–whether the higher revenue collected reflects the fee for larger acreage or higher rates charged for a smaller area. This does point to the caution required

TABLE 5.4: Statement of Collections of Water Charges for the Year 01-07-1998 to 15-05-1999

(Rupees)

Mandal	Arrears			Current (Kharif)			Current (Rabi)			Total balance due*
	Demand as on 1-7-98	Collections	Balance due	Demand	Collection	Balance due	Demand	Collections	Balance due	
Miryal-guda	180,97,597	6,53,593	174,44,004	58,58,180	37,62,278	20,95,902	35,15,750	nil	35,15,750	230,55,656

Source: Mandal Revenue Office, Miryalguda, District Nalgonda

*Against a total due balance of more than 2.3 crores the collections have been only Rs. 45 lacs.

to the caution required to interpret the statistics. And simple *claims of higher revenues* are not necessarily reflective of higher rate of fee collection. It can, in fact *conceal* lower rate of fee collection. The point is that these issues cannot be sorted out *a priori* but has to be analysed further in-depth for which disaggregated data is required.

The second cause of low revenue collections is the mis-reporting of revenue, which has actually been collected. There exists a strong bias on the part of the revenue personnel for under reporting the area irrigated by revenue department. This leads to lower reported acreage and thus, the need to deposit smaller amounts of revenue, (which might have in fact been collected) in the treasury. It works as follows: if a farmer owns 'x' acres of land, he pays revenue for 'x-a' acres only on the understanding that it is not entered in the official records. Such an arrangement is mutually beneficial to the Village Administrative Officer (VAO) who is the local collecting authority as representative of the revenue department and the farmer. While the former pockets the collection, the latter has to part with fewer funds. This would also depress the financial returns, to the irigation department, as they are proportional to irrigated area. Therefore, the reason for low returns is three fold—one, due to under-reporting by revenue department data collectors i.e. VAOs; two, due to non-compliance by water users as a result of poor water service delivery and consequent lack of motivation to pay their dues; and three, due to non-payment inspite of getting more than their due share of water due to weak collection systems.

Recently the department has initiated a policy of conducting a 'joint *azmaish*' i.e. a combined assessment by four persons one each from the department of agriculture, irrigation and revenue and the local WUA office bearer. This is a welcome development and is gradually being implemented in more and more areas under canal commands. However, there is a resistance to the grounding of this method of assessment of area irrigated by the local revenue person as it threatens their ability to manipulate statistics. The field engineers cited many instances of a stalemate between the two departments. In such situations the irrigation department and dry does not sign the joint *azmaish*. It is, however, the revenue figures, which are entered, in the official records by the bureau of economics and statistics and is considered the authoritative figure by the Chief Planning Officer for the purpose of development planning. There is thus, a significant discrepancy between the data on area irrigated from the two sources. See Table 5.5 for a comparison of data for the same area from two sources i.e. revenue department and ID.[1]

Even if the joint assessment is conducted with cooperation of the concerned departments—there is the further question of *what counts* as area irrigated. Is it single, double or requisite number of irrigation? The quality of irrigation for which the area is assessed should also be recorded—since the ability and inclination to pay the water cess depends on that to a large extent. This is a critical point to which the government agencies are yet not sensitive. The concept of area irrigated has to be clearly defined and there has to be a commonly accepted understanding.

From the perceptions of the farmers surveyed it was found, that there was no resistance to paying higher charges for water. This was particularly true of farmers from among the medium to small landowners who were at the tail end. The important condition of payment was the dependability of the irrigation service. As of now, although expectations are raised, there is little likelihood of the tail areas getting the water due to them. During periods of water scarcity, economically powerful and socially influential landowners could partly compensate their discriminatory access to water by organizing a patrol party to monitor illegal withdrawals upstream of their lands. However, this was not always successful and quite cumbersome. An easier option was to install their own borewells provided it was technologically feasible. In either case, payment of water cess from them is bound to be negligible. Increasing water rates will by itself provide little relief to the public exchequer. Table 3.1 also indicates that significant payment of water cess continues at the old rates.

The burden of water tax to the farmer is not at all high, atleast in the relative sense. From the cost of production data collected for a small sample of farmers, it was found that water cost, as per

TABLE 5.5: Total Area Irrigated (Canals) in all the villages under distributary according to MRO and Department data (hectares)

WAZEERABAGH DISTRIBUTARY

Year	Kharif						Rabi					
	MRO			DEPT			MRO			DEPT		
	WET	ID	T	WET	ID	T	WET	ID	T	WET	ID	T
1989												
1990				8541	3361	11902				3304	5620	8924
1991				7290	758	8048				na	na	na
1992				7316	3670	10986				1319	-	1319
1993				7263	1270	8533				5236	3181	8417
1994				7452	2181	9633				6162	1595	7757
1995	7400	3	7403	6900	-	6900	3692	825	4517	na	na-	na
1996	6841	-	6841	8000	-	8000	696	14	710	3000	4050	7050
1997	7139	53	7192	8000	400	8400	2366	1174	3540	200	9000	9200
1998	7467	-	7467	6800	2552	9352	356	13	369	150	2140	2290
1999	7733	4	7737	8900	1823	10723	4511	155	4666	9000	2000	11000

Source: Computed from Division Offices and RDO offices from Karimnagar & Miryalguda..

for a small sample of farmers, it was found that water cost, as per the new rates, amounted to a maximum of 5% of the total annual paid out costs of production. (See Table 5.6). This is of the same order as for the Mexican programme of PIM, where the corresponding figure varied between 3% to 5% (Johnson: 1997). The monthly cost of water per acre would work out to be not more than Rs. 20. Thus it is not the 'high' rates *per se* which might depress the revenue collections and eventual sustainability. Rather it is the effective delivery of the water to the tail areas—a categorically stated objective of the PIM reforms. This in turn provides the basis of insisting on better compliance to terms of payment. Evidence from Table 3.1 shows that respondents were very categorical about payment of water fees only if they get a good service. Few were also critical of the new enhanced rates as not being justified by any increase in productivity. For the majority, however, it was *not the high rate but poor irrigation* that was a matter of concern.

Cost of Production (COP)

COP data was collected for the random sample of farmers from head, middle and tail areas surveyed (see Table 5.6) Data was collected only for paid out costs of inputs and actually sold outputs. The rice output, therefore, excludes the output, which is typically retained for domestic consumption. This was done with a view to assessing the net surplus accessible in fact to the cultivator, after ensuring his survival. Similarly, labour costs did not include imputed values for family labour. It was felt that it is the cash costs and returns that bear significantly on immediate production decisions of a farmer. Secondly, if water cess was not being paid then the farmer did not count it as a cost. During discussions with the farmers cost of water irrespective of the fact whether it was paid or not—never emerged as an important issue it was the availability and access to water that were problematic.

Evidence from COP Data

1. Cropping intensity is lower under tanks and at tail end areas of

TABLE 5.6: Cost of Production Data For Canals and Tanks

System	Location On the system (Head, Middle of Tail)	Land size (acres)	Water cost as a % of total production cost	Income per month per acre	Main crops grown R (rice), M (maize), C (cotton) (T (turmeric), G (groundnut), Ch (chillies)
NSP	H	4	2	479	R
		4	2	589	R
		6	2	481	R
		6	*	136	R
	M	4	*	189	R
		1.5	4	133	R
		18	*	1402	R + C + Ch
	T	6	*	1590	R + C + Ch
		3	*	549	R + Ch
		18	1	302	R + G + M + T
SRSP	H	5	1	446	R + G + M + T
		3	3	285	R + T + M
		3	4	89	R
	M	5	1	446	R
		16	2	724	R + M

(Contd.)

TABLE 5.6: *(Contd.)*

System	Location On the system (Head, Middle of Tail)	Land size (acres)	Water cost as a % of total production cost	Income per month per acre	Main crops grown R (rice), M (maize), C (cotton) (T (turmeric), G (groundnut), Ch (chillies)
		1.5	3	117	M
	T	4	*	493	R + M
		10	1	167	R + T+ M
		3	1	988	R + T
TANKS	H	4	3	316	R + G+ T+ C
		5	2	344	R + T
		2	*	-12.5	R
	M	3	8	228	R
		6	2	593	R + T
		2	*	471	R + T
	T	2	7	- 197	R
		5	5	369	R + T+ G

Source : Data collected during fieldwork in 1998-99;

* Water dues not paid; R-rice; C-cotton; Ch-chillies; M-maize; G- groundnut; T-turmeric

canal irrigation, which is also corroborated by the other sample (see Tables 4.2, 4.3 and 4.4).

2. Rice cultivation in tail areas is possible only with an alternative source of irrigation—usually a well from where water is pumped out using an electric motor.
3. Farmers at tail end who cannot resort/do not have the option of a well, operate at survival levels.
4. Most farmers at the tail reaches of the source do not pay water cess. This is also corroborated by the data in the main sample.
5. Water charges when paid do not comprise more than 5% of the total paid out annual costs of production for agricultural activity.
6. Highest cash income per acre per month is concentrated in the tail area of NSP which are totally dependent on well irrigation and grow a combination of irrigated dry cash crops such as Cotton and Chillies that are very lucrative (see Table 5.6). Small farmers (in box in the above Table) under tanks and without wells of their own, and cultivating rice for self-consumption had negative incomes. Pure rice cultivators in the middle reaches under NSP had lowest incomes. While the data is too limited to provide a basis for a definite hypothesis, it does point to possible areas for further investigation *e.g.* comparison of costs of production of only rice cultivation and when the total package includes high profitability crops like Cotton, Chillies and Turmeric. Secondly, the plight of small farmers at the tail end who grow rice for self-consumption needs to be weighed against water wastage at the head due to commercial cultivation of rice.
7. In addition, the smaller farmers were possibly constrained by timely access to other inputs due to credit constraints. However, data on access to credit was not collected during fieldwork. The inference of scale bias in access to credit can only be based on secondary data at macro level (see Rao, 1994). However, it is very unlikely to encounter the case of even a small farmer where inspite of the availability of water production of lucrative cropping pattern is *not* undertaken due to lack of credit. Profitability may be reduced for the small farmer due to onerous

terms of credit relative to resource rich farmers. But production could be undertaken due to the relative advantage of intensive family labour. The latter can however, compete with HYV technology as a source of increase only to a limited extent–i.e. to the extent that the labour process of cultivating a particular crop is labour intensive.

8. Financial returns from irrigated dry crops such as chillies, cotton and turmeric were high, but variation in their yield was also higher. For instance the total output per acre for turmeric could vary from Rs. 10,000 to Rs. 50,000.
9. Rice being the main staple diet of the community explains its preponderance among cultivators, even in the poorest households. Second reason for preference for rice was the high yield variation of other irrigated dry crops inspite of their higher profitability as noted above. In addition, these crops also required heavy investment for inputs. The financial risk in case of low outputs was relatively higher in their case—constraining their wider adoption.

Maintenance and Operation (M&O)

Discussions on poor M&O in the literature are typically discussed purely in financial term—with the *physicality* and *timeliness* of maintenance not accorded its due recognition for its impact on the requirement of financial resources as well as utilisation of the existing/available resources. A welcome departure from this was the collaborative study conducted by IIMI (Colombo) & IIM (Ahmedabad) on the impact of irrigation management transfer to the WUAs. With reference to maintenance they find that inspite of similar average annual expenditures on maintenance on the transferred and non-transferred minors in their sample, the performance of the transferred minors was distinctly better. The explanation for the difference lies "in the way maintenance was managed ..... the irrigation department prefer to desilt and clean whole minor at one time every few years rather than clean and desilt small portions each year.... Also irrigation department employees tend to spend little time on any particular canal or canal section, resulting in relatively low knowledge of detailed maintenance needs" (Maharashtra IMT impact Assessment, 1999). This reinforces the point made later about better maintenance possible with same quantum of funds or similar output with smaller funds. That is, it is the inefficiency of use of given funds that determine the quality of maintenance.

This is not to discount the need for minimum financial resources. The root cause of poor levels of maintenance lies more often in the inefficient utilisation of this resource. The impact assessment study of the Mexican programme of PIM also underscores the noticeable improvement in maintenance of the system consequent on the transfer of management to the users. Not only has the quality of maintenance improved, it has been achieved with fewer staff and at declining cost. The focus of maintenance has shifted from main canal to the terminal end of the system. These effects were corroborated by the perceptions of the farmers (Johnson, IIWI, 1997). In AP the recent attempts are focusing on all-round maintenance since condition of the entire system was in a bad shape. While the irrigation department is managing the main system rehabilitation, the institutional network of farmers' representatives is reconditioning the terminal network beyond distributaries.

If routine maintenance is done regularly to keep the system in good shape and continuous monitoring identifies any weaknesses that are developing, it can be checked in the initial stages and major breakdowns can be prevented. This has significant cost saving consequences for the maintenance budget. If, however, the system is allowed to deteriorate to the extent of absolute breakdown—then there is no choice but to go in for high cost repair and maintenance options. The technological options/choices for maintenance are a function of ongoing maintenance. Insufficient allocation of funds for such routine maintenance, therefore, turns out to be very expensive in the long run.

The second issue is of utilisation of available funds for ongoing maintenance by the irrigation agencies with the usual bureaucratic constraints and inefficiencies. In this context handing over the management to locally elected bodies of the users is a very powerful mode of enhancing financial efficiency and can entail tremendous improvement in quality of works done. It is not surprising, therefore, that the most impressive and immediate outcome of the reforms is in the field of works undertaken for repair and rehabilitation, which is physically apparent even to a casual visitor.

Ample evidence was available for this from field visits during the first phase of minor repairs being carried out on the minors and distributaries. The main works are the following: removal of silt, clearing of weeds and vegetation repair of structures and sluices, closing of breaches, repair of canal banks, repair of drops etc. The single most important development is the fact, that local works are being carried out without the intervention of contractors from outside. The entire exercise is managed by the interaction with the Competent Authority (CA), who is a department engineer, and the WUA office bearers. Right from identification of works to be undertaken, preparation of estimates by the CA, release of funds in a phased manner by the Pay & Accounts department after sanction by the Superintending Engineer. The department gives monitoring and technical support and conducts periodic inspections. The government has allocated Rs. 100 per acre as maintenance grant to WUAs, and an additional amount to DCs. Therefore, this year (i.e. 1998-99) a total of Rs. 200 per acre grant has been allocated for maintenance to the PIM bodies as a 100% subsidy by government during the first year, to be followed by 66-2/3% in the second year and 33 1/3% in the third year. It is in the fourth year that the farmers will have to depend entirely on their own resources. During the first year money has in fact, reached and works are going on in full swing and concurrently. This is not only more effective in terms of total amount of work output but also has lower financial leakage and more efficient use of the funds. The users have a direct stake in better quality work and there is greater financial transparency. Some farmers did make cynical comments about the contractors becoming WUA presidents or these presidents operating like contractors. While this may be true, it is still better to have a contractor from the same or nearby village as he is likely to be more accountable to the farmers and has a vested interest in doing a better job compared to a total outsider. Secondly, since the positions are elected, the members of WUA always have the option of not re-electing the errant candidates. The situation may not be ideal in these respects but does constitute a distinct improvement over the earlier condition.

The greatest obstacle to the smooth functioning comes from the Pay & Accounts section of the department. There is a widespread feeling among the farmers that they expect bribes for a speedy processing of the papers. This is also confirmed by the regular feedback conducted by the IB. (Saddassu feedback 1998, 1999) Systematic complaints of such nature are not made regarding other officers. In fact there was considerable evidence of cordial relations with the CA—the nodal officer dealing with the WUA officers. Occasional instances of conflict came to the fore. (TH, 1998). By and large however, interaction with the CAs did not emerge as a serious problem, even when the farmers were deliberately questioned about this (See Table 3.1)

While recognising the positive impact of PIM on maintenance of the irrigation channels, which were in a bad shape, there arises one basic question i.e. can the system survive if the continuous flow of funds comes to halt? Recent government pronouncements have proposed that the entire water fee collected would be diverted to the WUAs as their maintenance grant. Even the fee collection responsibility would be handed over to them. As of now the fee is collected by the VAO. Field survey points to a tremendous *resistance* to fee collection responsibility by the WUA presidents and TC members. Their argument is as follows—being elected representatives they have no authority to impose the payment of water charges due to fear of incurring their wrath in case farmer refuses to pay. They have no way of ensuring compliance. If they use any pressure they run the risk of earning unpopularity among the users—which will be reflected in their being thrown out as office bearers. The farmers were therefore very reluctant to accept this responsibility. Whether their apprehensions are valid or not—can only be tested after actual implementation. Secondly, if it is proposed to finance all future maintenance through the water fee

Rs. 200 per acre which are equal to what is being spent now) are not adhered to. Already there is lot of resistance to the proposal of farmer contribution for WUA funds. In order to elicit financial contribution from users, ground level mobilisation and motivation are very important. A degree of transparency at the level of general body of water users and confidence of user control over water supply has to be established for convincing them to comply with their financial obligations. As of now, grass-root interventions are conspicuous by their absence. How then is the financial self-sufficiency proposed to be ensured such that the level of maintenance can be sustained? The question of *financial sustainability of WUAs* in the absence of external inflow of resources is very critical and needs to be faced squarely.

Table 5.7 shows the order of financial commitment for the irrigation sector from domestic and international sources. Although continuation of external funding is contemplated for both the new and ongoing schemes, it still leaves open the question of financial viability of the entire irrigation organisation. While there is a justification for some form of subsidy for the capital expenditure for irrigation investment, as is the case all over the world including developed countries (see Chapter 7), atleast the recurring costs of reproducing the service over time are required to be met through revenue generation. It may be pointed that success of the Mexican programme is critically dependent on its financial self-sufficiency. Johnson's study of the irrigation management transfer in Mexico

TABLE 5.7: Sources and Financial Outlays for two-year action plan (1998-2000) for irrigation

World Bank (AP III APERP, Hazard Mitigation)	Rs. 1990 crores
OECF Japan (KC canal modernisation)	Rs. 550 crores
Rural Infrastructure Development Fund (NABARD)	Rs. 500 crores
Accelerated Irrigation Benefit Programme (AIBP)	Rs. 542 crores
Bonds Money	Rs. 370 crores

Source: White Paper on Irrigation 1997.

Johnson's study of the irrigation management transfer in Mexico points out that "..... water user associations have proven capable of operating and maintaining the modules, even upto sizes in excess of 50,000 hectares, and water fees collected by the users have not only supported the module O & M activities but have also funded most of O & M activities by CAN staff at the main canal and water source levels. This is in sharp contrast to the situation that existed when the systems were heavily dependent upon government subsidies and consequently were deteriorating rapidly due to lack of stable funding." (Johnson, 1998). The fee recovery from the modules was sometimes more than 100%—i.e. they often paid the fee in advance of the required time, which was before the delivery of irrigation water. That the same may be possible in case of Andhra Pradesh by charging water rates which do not exceed 5% of the cost of production of the farmers, point to the realistic feasibility of self-sufficiency in terms of M & O expenses. Absence of this will continue to result in a drain on the public exchequer. This would put pressure for cuts elsewhere or possibly a weakening of M & O leading to deterioration of the system, which is going back to square one.

NOTE

1. It is extremely tedious to generate this comparison since data from revenue department is collected according to the revenue village boundaries, whereas the irrigation department collects it according to the distributary command area contours. The two need not coincide. Therefore, data for each of the villages under the distributary was collected from revenue records and added to arrive at a commensurable figure. Some of the villages are irrigated by more than one distributary. In such a case, approximations of proportion of area irrigated by each distributary are used to consider only that proportion of total revenue accruing due to irrigation by that distributary. The total of all the villages thus arrived at is then compared with the data from irrigation department for that particular distributary.

6

PIM AND INSTITUTIONAL CHANGES

The major institutional issue *vis-a-vis* the irrigation reforms that excites curiosity and evokes interest is the nature and extent of participation that the reforms have succeeded in realising with particular reference to the initial objectives. The fundamental understanding of the malaise afflicting the performance of the public irrigation projects was the managerial inefficiency. The technical, financial, water use efficiency and productivity problems associated with irrigation projects were rooted not so much in lack of resources or know-how. Rather it was the poor overall performance inspite of not being constrained by the above factors. While shortage of finances is often cited as a limiting parameter, the argument does not carry weight given the high degree of investments done in irrigation sector during the successive plan periods representing 23 to 36% of total plan outlay. (See Table 6.1) and amounting to a total of Rs. 5250 crore.

Various attempts had also been made in the preceding decades to provide know-how through extension coupled with credit support at the grass-root level by programmes such as CADA without, however, much success on a sustainable level. The irrigation department had been unable to maintain either the main system or the terminal network of supply channels. The water distribution rules and regulation were flouted more as a routine rather than exception and had lost all meaning. Within this backdrop, and motivated possibly by external circumstances and pressures (abstracting from them for the present), the irrigation reforms—

with a focus on users participation in the M & O of the irrigation system—were instituted in AP about two years ago. The underlying expectation was first, to systematise water distribution and second to improve the terminal level of supply channels by decentralising their upkeep and maintenance through shifting its responsibility to organised groups of users. This, as argued earlier, was perceived to be a more efficient management strategy. Since the water users are spread out in space it is practically convenient to allow them to handle micro level distribution of water among them, while the irrigation department is entrusted with the responsibility of providing water in a lumpsum at head of the channels. Devolution of responsibility had to go hand in hand with the devolution of authority to take decisions. This is the crux of participation that is envisaged i.e., the facility to take decisions regarding the *distribution of water* and the *maintenance* of distribution network of water channels. With this in mind, organisations of water users were formed and the rest is history.

Two pre-requisites for the participation as above to be viable are one, the availability of financial resources with the WUAs on a sustainable basis for M&O and two, the ability of WUAs to *implement* the rules of water distribution which are democratically agreed upon. To begin with financial grants have been allocated to WUAs and DCs for initiating the long overdue and urgently

TABLE 6.1: Plan Outlays on Irrigation Schemes

(Rs. Crores)

Plan period	Total plan	Irrigation outlay	Percentage
I Plan	96.78	21.85	22.50
II Plan	188.60	65.54	34.75
III Plan	352.41	124.48	35.53
IV Plan	448.87	124.96	27.80
V Plan	1444.71	456.18	31.57
VI Plan	3237.07	867.40	26.80
VII Plan	5976.60	1434.69	24.70
VIII Plan	10500.00	2500.00	23.80

Source: Factual Note: Irrigation Sector, 1997, GOAP

required repairs to the irrigation structures. As noted earlier, significant and commendable work has been completed and is continuing as a result of this intervention. Although it is easy to find faults with progress of activities being undertaken, the fact that a wide range of constructive activity which is *need* based, is being carried out simultaneously over a vast area on a scale never witnessed before, should not be lost sight of. What is even more striking is the fact that this has resulted from a government initiated programme, which has its usual limitations of bureaucratic functioning.

The systematic and fair elections that were held on a single day for 10,000 WUAs further underscores the political will to entrench these reforms. Detailed route maps and list of instructions were prepared for the polling officers. Following observations were noted during brief survey of 10 WUAs in Nalgonda district carried out on the day of the elections covering both tank and canal irrigated areas:

- The turnout of voters was more than 75%.
- Although women voters comprised only10-15% of the total number of voters, their turnout was more than 90% of the total number of female votes.
- Most of the presidents elected unanimously, had land holdings of 10 acres and above.
- The larger the number of candidates for a particular position (President or TC) the smaller was the average size of land owned by the candidates.
- There was the instance of a 1.5 acre landowning woman who stood for a TC position and was actively campaigning for herself, with support of other women and men.
- Door to door canvassing, banners and loud speakers were the most important means of canvassing.
- By 12 o'clock more than 50% of the votes had been polled in some of the polling booths. Old women with walking sticks were also seen at the polling booths.

Following issues were most prominent in the voters' minds:

* Bringing water to the tail areas.
* Avoid water wastage.
* Repair of physical structures.
* Better management and distribution of water.
* Clarification or redefining of commands. As of now farmers who had not irrigated for years had voting rights while those who had been irrigating for the last 20 years were not recognised as being within commands and therefore were not eligible to vote.
* Closer relationship between electorate and their representatives is likely to facilitate better management and maintenance of irrigation sources.

Administrative Reforms

To enhance the effective implementation of provisions of the Act by streamlining the functioning of Irrigation department, following administrative reforms were also instituted:

- "Appointment of Project Administrators duly delegated with the powers of the Chief Engineers level to ensure speedy execution of works and cutting-short of time delays.
- Creation of the posts of Districts Coordination in all districts to act as a liaison among the irrigation department and the Water Users Association.
- Enhancement in the powers of Executive Engineers and Superintending Engineer to accord technical sanctions to plan works upto Rs. 40 lacs and Rs. 100 lacs.
- Delegation of the powers of Commissionerate of Tenders to the Chief Engineers to finalise tenders for works upto Rs. 100 lacs.
- Delegation of powers to the Collectors to approve DN and DD I order to expedite land acquisition proceedings and to publish the same in all local newspapers and in the event of necessity to engage services of private surveyors.

- Permission to Project Administrators to engage private agencies for carrying out investigation works in case of need to expedite execution of works.
- Disposal of all surplus machinery available in the projects to realise revenues to the state. Government has also initiated steps to close the Mechanical workshops, which have become obsolete and redundant.
- Reformation and simplification of tender procedures in order to curb intimidation in filing of tenders and other malpractice. To encourage good contractors who execute public works qualitatively and within time, shall in future be issued merit certificates and will be given preference while giving works on nominations.
- Appointment of an advisor on Quality control to enforce prescribed quality control standards I the execution of works by all the engineering departments of the government.
- Integration of operations and maintenance of the wing of SRS project with that of Command Area Development and Construction wings to provide single point service to farmers.
- Creation of AP Water Resources Development Corporation for mobilising funds for the expeditious completion of ongoing projects.
- The government has also planned to make extensive use of information Technology to make the Irrigation department efficient, transparent and responsive to the needs of the farmers. The AP Irrigation Information System envisages a comprehensive basin wide network, linking major reservoirs for accessing real time data on water inflow and outflow, a canal management network and a construction module to closely monitor all aspects of project management. Wireless communication is being provided to all WUAs in the command of major projects to establish a close coordination between the farmers and irrigation officials to ensure timely, reliable and assured water supplies" (White Paper, 1997).

Participation of the WUAs (that is the president and/or

managing committee *only)* in the execution of the works is evidently manifest. We discuss below the question of participation by the *general body* separately. From the field observations it was found that all the works undertaken were identified by the elected bodies and also executed by them without the mediation of contractors or any other intermediary. The interaction was directly between the WUA and Competent Authority, who is from the irrigation department. There were well-defined channels of communication between user representatives and the irrigation agency i.e. irrigation department. That this communication network functioned effectively is also evident from the feedback obtained by the irrigation department where a majority of the presidents responded positively to their interaction with the irrigation department personnel. Compared to the prior anarchy and confusion in approaching the department for their problems, there now existed 'a single window'—the Competent Authority. He too had been given clear instructions and training about his role *vis-a-vis* the WUAs. The institutional structure of PIM has provided a forum for the users and the agency to come together and discuss irrigation issues—which was absent earlier. DCs have brought together farmers representatives from head and tail regions on a common platform. This is facilitating at least the *positing* of issues of discriminatory water availability across regions and its implications, especially during years of water scarcity. Whatever difficulties some WUAs experienced in accessing help from the department were more in the nature of teething troubles and could be expected to sort out in due course of time. Similarly the flow of funds to the WUAs was by and large satisfactory, if not perfect. In fact, it is this financial flow that singularly underlies the momentum that has currently been generated.

The second pre-condition i.e. the ability of WUAs to institute water distribution according to well-defined rules has been relatively difficult to achieve. This can be explained in the context of excessive preoccupation with paddy cultivation in the region, which engenders correspondingly heavy demand of water leaving little surplus for the downstream farmers. The latter in turn default on their payments of water dues. Most often they are not assessed for water fee payment. This response threatens sustainability of the reform initiatives. Government records also corroborate this. "Farmers in the head reaches of major and medium irrigation schemes are drawing water far in excess of their allocation and as a consequence, water is not flowing to tail areas. The problem is particularly acute in new commands which are based on ID cropping pattern and where farmers are resorting to paddy cultivation" (Factual Note, 1997: 98). The availability of financial resources as of now was not problematic. Clearly external flow of funds cannot continue indefinitely. Ultimately WUAs are conceptualised as financially self-sufficient entities for ensuring sustainability of the PIM framework. In order to achieve this, the water cess raised from within the commands of individual WUA is proposed to be handed over to them eventually for managing their total administrative and work related expenses. As a short-term measure to facilitate the transition, the government proposes to continue external funding but only in proportion to the water cess collected in the command of respective WUAs. This is visualised as an incentive for WUAs to ensure better compliance with payment of water dues.

We have noted earlier the widely prevalent tradition of defaulting on payments for water charges. How effectively, if at all, the WUAs counter this practice, constitutes the critical challenge for institutionalised 'participation'? How and to what extent are the WUAs going to discharge their responsibility of ensuring the payment of water cess is yet to be seen. What aspect of reforms has contributed to the acceptance of WUAs by the general body as authoritative institutions empowered to insist on payment of water dues—something that is a departure from previous practice? During fieldwork we have noted the reluctance of some WUAs to undertake this task as they run the risk of earning social ire. The extant system of collections through VAOs has been wrought with problems. There was very little in the field to suggest the emergence of a trend to mitigate the situation. Evidence illustrating continuing default on payments even in head reaches has been pointed out above.

This raises the issue of relationship between WUA managing

committee and its general body. How representative are these organisations? What is their social and political base? What is the extent of control/respect that they command within their jurisdiction? On this depends their ability to execute their role as fee collectors. It may be noted that so far none of the local elected bodies are charged with function of collecting taxes, and if they are, it is seldom successful.[1] To a certain extent it can be argued that the ability of WUAs to provide and manage effective irrigation might enable them to command social respect and legitimacy, which in turn would earn them the social recognition be able to ground fee collection institutions. This in turn depends on how effective are the WUAs in *distributing* water—which is the major constraining resource for production in the areas under consideration.

We have discussed at length the problem of controlling and regulating water flow among individual cultivators. Although, it is agreed that water is to be distributed in proportion to the land cultivated, extensive violation of the norm was evident. This practice had entrenched itself to the extent that extra withdrawals of water by head reach users for paddy cultivation had become the norm and was no longer even considered as 'unauthorised'. Over time this practice had acquired a sort of social acceptance. While differential water access was prominent *between* jurisdictions of different WUAs, it was noticeable even *within* the jurisdiction. Illegal water drawals continued to persist after the reforms. WUAs were unable to control such malpractice to any significant extent. Therefore, while the channels for carrying the water were shaped up, the water they carried continued to be erratic.

The above situation reflected weak control of the WUAs over their command areas. This is not surprising, given the top down nature of the reforms and very little awareness at the grass-root level. In fact, most of the WUAs were single person dominated organisations, owing allegiance to one or the other political parties. From a brief survey done on the educational, political and economic background of the presidents of WUAs, it was found that each had distinct political affiliations, had some elementary education

TABLE 6.2: *Profile of WUA Presidents*

Item	*Categories*	*No.*
EDUCATIONAL BACKGROUND	Nil	2
	Upto class 7	8
	From class 8 to 12	15
	College level	3
	Total	28
LAND OWNED (acres)	0-5	6
	6-10	13
	11-20	8
	Above 20	1
	Total	28
POLITICAL AFFILIATION	TDP*	11
	CI#	15
	CPM^	2
	Total	28

Source: Field data collected during 1998-99.
* Telugu Desam Party
\# Congress – I
^ Communist Party (Marxist)

and were reasonably well off (see Table 6.2). There was a marked difference between the president and the other members of the managing committee in terms of their social and economic status. They were by and large subservient to the president. Most of them had very little information about the activities of the WUA or interaction with neighbouring WUAs or about the meetings of the DC. The awareness of the general body members was even less. Some farmers at the head reach areas had no idea about the programme. Although they did recall the event of elections to WUAs, it was a distant memory. Only 30% of the farmers surveyed knew the name of the president, hardly any one knew the names of managing committee members. Exceptions were certainly noticed of extremely enthusiastic and well known presidents of some WUAs and DC presidents e.g. the woman WUA president from distributary D89 on SRSP project as discussed in Chapter 7. The character of WUAs is similar to the Panchayati Raj institutions. Their effectiveness will depend on the extent to which a grass-root level awareness is generated regarding the entitlements of general body members and to the extent that general body members are organised to exert pressure for better services from these organisations. In other words, it is only grass root mobilisation for the activation of basic democratic processes that can lead to a greater responsiveness of WUAs to members of its general body. Wider dissemination about the PIM programme and its potential for enhancing efficiency, stability, incomes and productivity through innovative communication strategies is a necessary though not sufficient condition for grounding these reforms.

Mere publicity is not enough to realise greater effectiveness in institutionalising these reforms. Their practical viability depends on the ability to remove the root cause of out of turn water drawals, so as to bring about better adherence to rules of water distribution. As discussed earlier the need of excessive drawals of water is based in the widespread paddy cultivation prevalent in the area. Improvements in the delivery systems to facilitate volumetric pricing of water could be an alternative. This needs to be examined. In addition attempts could be directed at weaning farmers away from this cropping pattern, wherever possible. This could be tried by providing technological alternatives that are practically feasible and economically lucrative.

Effective control of water distribution is likely to facilitate higher revenue collections. As discussed above and illustrated by the field data, payment of water dues has typically been problematic. Reasons are twofold—one, default due to lack of pressure to pay inspite of getting water. Two, refusal to pay due to poor irrigation service provided or accessible. Added to this are the lower remittances by the local revenue department personnel. Efficient functioning of the system on a sustainable basis will have positive impact on the financial management by providing an incentive to pay. Financial inflows in turn will make possible the continuous maintenance of the system requiring fewer quanta of funds because of regular upkeep, as argued earlier. This is a critical requirement since the external funding support available at present cannot continue indefinitely.

Conclusion

From the foregoing discussion we can infer that the WUAs have performed very successfully as institutions for executing activities for improved maintenance and repair of the channels by accessing funds from the government. However, as regulatory institutions incharge of water distribution on equitable basis their performance has been quite weak and ineffective. This bears adversely on their ability to generate resources through collection of water cess. In the coming years this would seriously constrain the reproduction of WUAs as viable organisations. Technological interventions to improve delivery systems and provide realistic alternatives to high water consumption crops need to be undertaken to enable extensive spread of irrigation benefit rather than concentrate its benefits to the few. The latter would impair the financial sustainability of WUAs, thereby threatening their institutional viability.

NOTE

1. See UNICEF (1997) problems associated with tax collection by Gram Panchayats in Ranga Reddy district.

7

REVIEW OF ISSUES AND SUGGESTIONS

We have discussed above the consequences of irrigation reforms for agrarian development, under the command of two major irrigation projects in Andhra Pradesh. This raises issues of replicability and sustainability at a wider level, which have a bearing on the macro policy formulation. The Andhra experiment of instituting irrigation reforms is being watched with tremendous interest across the country. The problems it addresses are common and pertinent to other areas as well. However, a critical assessment of the experience must precede any attempt at emulation of the model. Below we discuss the potential and constraints of PIM as envisioned in AP, for realising irrigation induced development objectives.

Irrigation and Production

Increased production of output through irrigation is realised by an increase in area cultivated, increase in cropping intensity, increasing per acre outputs of individual crops, increasing total per acre productivity, and switch to less water consumptive cropping pattern. The total change in output consequent to changes in irrigation availability is net of the magnitude of the changes effected in the above variables. It is not necessary for these changes to be complementary and reinforcing and they could possibly counteract each other. Switch to more water consumption crop, induced by increased water availability, for instance, can lead to a reduction of net sown area or constrain its increase.

PIM in AP has led to marginal increase in Gross Area Irrigated (GIA) and area cultivated as already discussed in context of the field areas. This has been possible due to increased water availability to limited number of downstream farmers resulting from technical improvement effected in the supply channels. The correlation of higher irrigated acreage associated with greater number of better quality of irrigation sources is also corroborated for the different regions of the state as a whole. Since rice is the major crop in irrigated areas and PIM efforts are necessarily directed to areas that are already endowed with irrigation facilities with the objective of improving their efficiency, most of this increase in area irrigated has been absorbed by rice cultivation. As such, the existing bias of irrigation investment towards high water consumption cropping pattern is reinforced. This is typically at the expense of other crops like oilseeds, pulses, maize etc., which are starved of even their lower water demands. If cultivated, the latter set of crops could extend irrigation to a larger acreage.

It may be noted that extensive use of land and water generates higher green cover, fewer disturbances to the ecological balance, more employment from work on larger landmass and greater production of total biomass. The tradeoff between intensive and extensive cultivation depends on the availability and cost of reclaiming uncultivated land. However, under the existing economic environment in an already well-endowed area, the individual producer finds it more rational to allocate increased irrigation resource to rice cultivation. This may lead to inefficient resource (land and water) use efficiency at the macro level by foregoing some of the advantages outlined above.

Field observations at the farm level point to a tendency towards an increase in Net Sown Area (NSA), Cropping Intensity (CI) and Gross Irrigated Area (GIA). This implies that while additional area has been brought under cultivation there has also been a switch to rice cultivation to the extent warranted by increased water availability. The total output would also increase in proportion to the increase in GIA. This increase is largely confined to the farmers in the middle reaches who are the ones who have benefited most from the supply side efficiencies in water delivery. The head end farmers, large to small, have had sufficient water throughout, while the tail end farmers have not still received their due share. Thus, there has been little change in their situation.

There is as yet, no evidence of a *change* in per acre yields of rice among any category of water users. Yield levels attained are the net result of a complex set of variables e.g. fertiliser use, timeliness and control of water application. It may be noted that use of fertiliser is highly elastic to variations in its own price relative to expected quantum and price of output. Secondly, the marginal productivity of fertiliser declines with high level of fertiliser application, eventually becoming negative. It is the most significant factor for explaining yield differentials. However, yield response of fertiliser depends critically on controlled supply of water. Intensive water use due to subsidised pricing and at a flat rate system of charging results in declining marginal cost of water (as also the average cost) with increasing use. This, coupled with absence of technical control structures encourages inefficient water use at field level. The most serious consequence of such mode of water use is that it compromises efficiency of other inputs as well. Inefficient water utilisation therefore induces inefficiency of complementary input use. Subsidised water pricing in addition taps on financial resources, which have competitive demands for alternative development ventures. It may be noted however, that the increased water availability due to PIM reforms need not necessarily manifest itself in increasing intensity of cultivation or reinforcing water consumptive cropping pattern. It so happens to be the case in A.P. due to prevailing delivery systems where volumetric release and pricing of water is not possible. This calls for major reforms in the delivery systems.

In the light of the overall tendency of PIM reforms to reinforce rice cultivation under the prevailing water delivery and pricing systems, there is a strong need to institute policy measures to partially counteract the trend and stimulate production of low water use crops and water conserving agricultural practices. This requires both market and non-market interventions, as discussed below.

It is important to institute these measures in the beginning itself, because once rice cultivation gets entrenched in an area, the flexibility of response of the cultivator is constrained partly due to the particular soil water balance that is established. It is for this very reason why rice cultivators in some areas find it difficult to switch to dry land crops during years of drought.

Stability

In this context, the consequences of PIM programme in AP, for its impact on stabilising output assume significance. We have discussed above the stimulus given to rice cultivation through an increase in area, not yield, as a result of the reforms. In the first two years of implementing the reforms, the rainfall has been relatively plenty. It is, therefore, difficult to isolate the impact of reforms on reducing variation in the output of rice. However, among the HYV crops commonly grown in the region, rice has been observed to have a higher sensitivity to variations in rainfall (Rao, 1994).

We have already discussed above the poor *control* over water distribution by downstream/midstream farmers that has been observed in the field areas. This is not a managerial or administrative problem that will be taken care of "in due course of time". Underlying this is the hard-core economic conflict arising out of discriminatory control over water resources. Hence, it is an observation that cannot be explained by the initial stage of the programme but derives from the very nature of the interventions. It is the inability to redistribute water equitably among the head and tail end farmers and its continuing monopoly by upstream water users, that constitutes the basis of uncertainty of water supply as you go downstream. Even if certainty and assurance of a given quantum were there—the major crop being rice, coping up with water shortage during low rainfall years would be problematic. We have already noted above the technical difficulty of switching back and forth from rice cultivation. The land in a sense gets "addicted" to the rice crop. The fluctuations in output for the downstream farmers get amplified, accentuating instability due to purely climatic factors. As a result cultivators experience greater vulnerability based on locational disadvantage. PIM reforms were expected to result in a greater certainty of supply, which as of now appears a remote possibility.

Equity

There have been attempts to circumvent marginalisation of tail areas by the irrigation department by introducing a system of rotation of canal water supplies. However, such attempts are not very successful at counteracting the bias. This is also corroborated from evidence on the changes due to PIM in the field areas. The simultaneous existence of inefficient resource use at head end with its scarcity at the tail end of the same channel (approximately 30 Kms) has serious implications for growth, equity, stability and efficiency. During a high rainfall year of 1998 (when the fieldwork was conducted), the head reach farmers were drawing water for a second crop of rice and had a bumper crop. At the same time, there was visible anger and helplessness among the tail end farmers due to water shortage even for their dry crops. There is a strong case for redressing this imbalance by suitable control of water distribution and ensuring its effective implementation. A simple and easy to implement rule of water distribution is to start water supply from tail and proceed backwards to head reach farmers. As the flow of water is reduced towards the end of a watering cycle, it can irrigate areas close to the outlet more efficiently than areas further away. This system has been implemented in isolated cases as was observed in a distributary on the Koyal Sagar dam in Mahabubnagar district but with high degree of success, apparently due to the efforts of a very motivated junior engineer from the irrigation department. Such examples need to be replicated and supportive government policy should be co-opted as a part of the PIM strategy.

An option suggested to overcome the scale/fragmentation problem of scattered holdings is to redistribute small-holdings in a cluster (Rao, 1994). This would facilitate the provision of irrigation on a collective basis and reduce supply inefficiencies.

Finally, NGOs can be involved to mobilise the community of water users for optimum utilisation of a common resource such as water. Awareness about alternative cropping patterns with reduced water demands and comparable economic returns can be disseminated through practical demonstrations, to motivate the head reach farmers to comply with commonly accepted rules of water distribution.

It is pertinent to note that farmers at the head reaches will not *voluntarily* give up an advantage (however unfair) that they have become accustomed to. It would be politically unattractive for any government to enforce such compliance by force. In addition to reforming delivery systems in tune with decentralised management, the only realistic strategy of weaning them away from water intensive cultivation is to conduct model demonstration *at the field level* and on a *turnkey basis* of total production packages possible under those agro-climatic conditions. Focus should also be given to ensuring the availability of inputs and existence of market for the output.

Technological Feasibility of PIM

PIM programme aims at a decentralised management of the irrigation systems. This involves a greater devolution of decision-making powers to the local organisation along with greater authority and responsibility. However, these institutional reforms would require corresponding reforms in the technical design and concept of the projects—particularly of the distribution system. Most of the projects inherit the design rationale from the colonial period, when the imperative of *central* control of water distribution and revenue collection was paramount. Institutional restructuring which proposes to reverse the pattern of control and responsibility requires technical interventions to make the changes viable. For instance, the critical innovation of user's control over the distribution of water would require his control over supply of water as well. This would not be easy to achieve unless a decentralisation of storage structures was created as well. In fact, dispersed storage structures with smaller conveyance networks are more efficient as they entail lower transit losses. Ensuring equity in distribution, as argued by Satnarayan Singh, a senior irrigation consultant on irrigation in AP, is not merely a "management problem requiring software solutions ... attention has not been given to hardware problems. None of the existing irrigation systems, as built, are capable of facilitating regulation and control needed to ensure equitable distribution of water amongst all the users. Everyone of the existing systems needs to be remodelled to secure fair distribution of water at various off-takes. This is an engineering deficiency......Before planning and designing the canal network with its various control structures, the operation plan of the system needs to be finalised keeping in view the objective of the project. The physical infrastructure should be planned, designed and built, to support the chosen operation plan. This has not been done for any of the existing irrigation schemes in the state. Operation and designs do not match. Nor any improved strategy is being adopted in designing new.schemes. Consequently there is and will be a mismatch in the controlling needs and system capabilities. As a result the type of distribution of water with focus on equity in sharing by different farmers regardless of their location in the system cannot be achieved."[1]

Alternative trajectories of water resource development need to be explored with a view to replacing lumpy investments with smaller scale and dispersed structures. This has corresponding implications for reduction in storage capacities and conveyance networks. It may be noted that percentage of water loss is in inverse proportion to the volume of water flow in the channels. Flow of water is lowest at the terminal level of the long network of channels under major projects. Lengthy distribution canals are therefore inefficient. Dispersal of storage structures and their smaller scale cause less violence to the environment. In addition, it enables greater flexibility and control by surrounding users to respond to their varying water requirements, as influenced by climatic fluctuations. This has implications for commensurate technical investments for ensuring technical feasibility.

Institutional Viability

Probably the most significant achievement of PIM reforms has been the creation of an institutional structure for channelling communication between the major stakeholders in the use of irrigation. Although, systems of management were existing hitherto but they were tardy, sluggish and inefficient. A bureaucracy weighed down with its procedural rules and regulations was slow to respond to the constant matching of irrigation supply with demands of a plethora of water users—spread out in space. To monitor innumerable micro level water distribution by a central organisation was indeed very inefficient. Chaotic management of water and other inputs required for realising the productive potential of water were manifesting themselves in poor yields and low irrigated acreage inspite of water release from the head works. It was in response to the coordination problems not only within the irrigation department, but also with other departments, that Command Area Development (CAD) was launched during the mid-70s in selected pockets of the country, including AP. However, the CADA approach only brought a number of officials from different departments under one organisation in a very eclectic manner. Cohesion or integration of efforts focused towards commonly accepted goals was missing. Few success stories such, as the experience in Pochampad area under the dynamic leadership of exceptionally committed officers like Mr. Hashim Ali, was more the exception that proved the rule. These success cases also crumbled soon after the concerned officers were transferred. An important weakness of the CADA programme was that the department was still dealing with a multitude of scattered farmers *at an individual level.* Secondly, it was still an approach of the government providing a service, *without any involvement of the users*. The decisions were taken by the agency and farmers were passive receivers. There was *no space for feedback* from the water users—no active role for them.

The significant departure that marks the initiation of PIM in AP is the creation of *organised* collectives of water users on one hand and a *single* nodal person the Competent Authority (CA) on the other hand. The communication line of an individual farmer through his WUA representatives with the government through CA—is simple, easily accessible and viable mode of mediating the interaction of a large number of farmers with the irrigation department. Dispersed farmers are efficiently integrated into the entire network through local departmental representatives.

Secondly, there is an explicit role for the water users in the management of M & O, conduct of minor repairs and water distribution in their respective areas. The idea is to make these organisations financially autonomous. The point is that there has been devolution of responsibility and decision-making powers—and this is a welcome step. Concurrently there is a concerted attempt to build up the capacity of the farmers for undertaking the management of irrigation at the local level. There is a massive training programme for skill development of the farmers being undertaken, regular feedback are conducted by having state level meetings of WUA presidents and DC presidents. This activity has generated a lot of interest and provoked lively discussions. So far, however, this interaction has been confined to the heads of the various organised units. Women participate to a limited extent—but the ones who do have come forward entirely on their own, without any special reservation. This is commendable since irrigation is traditionally a male dominated area.

In order to exploit the possibilities created by the novel institutional reforms, it is imperative to provide the cultivators concurrently with extension and credit support, particularly the weaker segments.

Economic Viability

We have noted from the secondary data and field observations that economic returns from the water charges collected are very poor. This is confirmed at the macro level for the state as a whole[2] as well as at the micro level from field investigations. Further evidence of financial inefficiency for the state as a whole is illustrated by the consistently high expenditure for major and medium projects on capital account, concomitant with near zero growth in area irrigated from 1980 to mid 90s (see Jairath, 1999).

Water availability is never a problem for the head reach farmers who nevertheless default on payments mainly due to weak collection mechanisms. Collection of fees is problematic from middle reach areas depending on the water actually received by them. It is, however, an acute problem towards the tail end. This is inspite of the willingness to pay the stipulated dues. It may be noted that the *reluctance to pay the water charges in large-scale canal irrigation projects is not related to the price of water.* Rather it is based on the *poor service of irrigation* provided. This is also confirmed by Vaidyanathan (1999) for the country as a whole. This is corroborated by the fact that inspite of the three to fourfold increase in water rates after PIM reforms —not a single protest was registered. Typically, such a sudden and drastic hike in the water charges would evoke strong, social and political protest. Of course this can partly be explained by poor compliance for payments, in which case raising the rates *per se* may be irrelevant. Fieldwork responses also confirmed the willingness of the farmers to pay their dues at the prevailing (and enhanced) rates provided they were assured of their due share of water. This was specifically true of the smaller farmers, reflecting their anxiety for getting water. There is little evidence to show that water users have withheld water use on account of high price inspite of availability. Water it may be noted is a pre-requisite for use of other inputs and its value to the user may far exceed its marginal product.

The overall poor financial performance of the irrigation sector was one of the strongest motivations for instituting PIM. Realising financial sustainability, especially at the WUA level is a major objective. However, this is also the most problematic aspect. Increased payment of higher water charges can be expected to come forth *only if* there is a radical improvement in the assured and timely water availability to the users. Water scarcity also has to be equally shared between location and class of farmers.

Maintenance and Operation (M&O)

The discussion relating to Maintenance and Operation (M&O) in official and academic literature is invariably reduced to questions of allocating more or less quantum of funds. This overlooks the basic issues of *how* the requirements for (M&O) are calculated and *what* are the institutional forms of conducting (M&O). As argued below it is the latter which influence the cost and efficiency of (M&O). *Maintenance is poor not because there are insufficient funds, but the funds are insufficient because the mode of maintenance (and fund utilisation) is poor.*

There are typically three kinds of maintenance required—preventive, upkeep and breakdown.[3] While the first two are conducted as a routine and on an ongoing basis, the last category of maintenance is required as and when a contingency arises. It requires major repairs, disruption of use and costs are significantly higher. Discourse on maintenance seldom distinguishes between these forms, which leads to confusion and misplaced emphasis on financial causes as the *only* reason for the widely observed poor maintenance of irrigation projects.

To begin with, the *need* for (M&O) is greater or lesser in proportion to the *quality* of irrigation works created (See Johnson *et al.*, 1997 for a similar discussion with reference to PIM in Mexico). Further, the quality of works follows more from the *mode* of utilising the financial resources and less from its absolute amount.

If users are involved in M & O in terms of having a control over the execution of works and expenditure of funds, and also share responsibility for conduct of the works, the outcome is likely to be more in tune with the field level requirements. The situations will in turn, encourage/motivate better payment of irrigation charges, costs of fee collection will be reduced due to pressure to pay up.[4] This brings us back to the basic point noted in the beginning, that the issues of *financial assessment, adequacy and efficiency of M&O* are very much rooted in the *institutional* context of creation and utilisation of irrigation works. The finances however, do present an outer boundary towards the attainment of possible levels of M&O. Identical amounts collected by different arrangements can have different implications for effective and timely M&O carried out.

It may be noted that *timely* and *regular* maintenance (preventive and upkeep) is highly cost effective as it reduces the need for *routine* maintenance. In addition, better upkeep of the system reduces the probability of major breakdowns. Thereby further reducing financial requirements. *Efficient maintenance self reinforces reduced requirement of financial resources*. On the other hand *mismanagement* of the execution of maintenance works *generates the need* for high cost of maintenance. The whole issue of shortage of financial allocation for maintenance is thus partly *artificially* generated.

It has been argued that decentralised M & O with greater user control at the local level would ensure: better quality of technical works, lower expenditure by cutting waste, increasing user involvement and lower supervision requirement.

The point is that financial resource required for M & O are *not a fixed and rigid quantum* given once for all with the objectivity of technological parameters. It is possible to have better quality of M & O with fewer resources, given alternative institutional environment.

In AP, users' participation in the rehabilitation and maintenance of the terminal level of the system constitutes the most effective, visible and significant consequence of PIM as noted above. Table 1.3 shows the works completed by WUAs for the state as a whole during the initial years of PIM, and the works in the pipeline. These are not merely government statistics. Field visits bear testimony to the fact of money actually reaching the WUAs and being utilised for physical works that are in fact being carried out with quality consciousness not found earlier. Secondly, the *pace* of work has gone up remarkably due to WUA involvement—the works are being undertaken simultaneously in a large number of projects. Since the funds are flowing in effectively, this part of the reforms has been extremely effective. This is truly remarkable considering that it is a government programme, wherein implementation is usually the weakest aspect. However, the 'operation' part of O & M continues to be problematic.

Irrigation Subsidies

The rationale of providing a subsidy derives from the desire to give economic support to resource poor users to facilitate their use of a particular commodity or service which has a high unit cost. Market prices are deliberately kept below efficient prices. However, as a price in the market it cannot discriminate between users of varying resource status. The relative advantage of the subsidy is, therefore, accessible to those with higher purchasing power. This may not create difficulty in case of commodities where slab pricing is possible with a flat rate for a minimum consumption for all and steeply graduated pricing for higher level of consumption as suggested by Vaidyanathan (1999). In case of subsidised pricing of public irrigation, however, it is not feasible to impose graduated price structure. Even recovery of the low water rates has been problematic, as discussed below. Graduated pricing would be next to impossible under the present system. This means that water availability is constrained not by pricing but by the fact of physical scarcity and localisation of supply. Therefore, while subsidy in case of public irrigation can throw open the market to all, concomitant market interventions to confine its advantage to poorer consumers is not possible. The net result is the disproportionately large benefits to the economically and locationally privileged water users.

It has been estimated that the proportion of input subsidy to agriculture, including irrigation for the country as a whole, has risen from 30% of the plan expenditure to nearly 90% during the 80s. Out of a total subsidy of nearly Rupees 14,000 crores during the decade, more than 10,000 crores were on account of irrigation alone (Rao, 1994 and Bhatia 1989). Most of this subsidy is for creation of irrigation potential and for providing subsidised water supply through *canals*. Given the regional bias in the spread of canal irrigation in the country and within AP (Jairath, 1999)[5], the subsidies too have a *regional* bias. Direct subsidies of public irrigation comprise the largest share of irrigation subsidies. Significant part of this public irrigation is used for HYV crops of wheat, rice and sugarcane.

The rising extent and uneven spread of subsidies across regions, sources and classes in the country, as a whole is a cause for concern. It has serious implications for accentuating inequity, which may be at the cost of foregoing productivity and income increases possible by extensive use of water. Subsidies concentrate water use to limited areas and crops. There too, subsidies encourage wasteful use of water, which is ironic given its scarcity and precious requirement by the small and downstream cultivators in the same region.

PIM strategy for reduction of indiscriminate subsidies is a welcome step. The *danger* in such a situation is that while the state absolves from the responsibility of maintenance and distribution of water and there is poor likelihood of the participatory institutions working out, the resource poor cultivators are at a total loss. Therefore, while subsidies may be reduced in the interest of efficient resource utilisation, adequate safety net and social security has to be provided to communities with precarious existence.

Reduction of subsidies raises the issue of fixation of irrigation fees, water rates etc. The criteria of fixing water charges have to be adopted in the context of overall policy financing of irrigation projects and the extent of subsidies, loans and recoveries expected or assumed underlying the investment decision.[6] Given the well-recognised benefits to the economy as a whole of irrigational development in a region, it has been argued that it is "inappropriate for the entire financial lenders to be borne solely by the farmers" (US Water Resource Policy Commission, 1950; 151). The question that arises is on what criteria is the water fees to be fixed; what proportion of costs of irrigation development is it expected to reimburse; should the recovery charges cover entire capital and O & M costs, or only entire O & M costs or only proportion of O & M costs. This constitutes the supply side criteria.

From the *users side*, should the criteria be fixed on the cost of irrigation or the ability to pay by the user or the incremental benefit derived by the user. It is for the government financing policies to opt for one or the other as a basis of assessment. It does however, point to the complexity of the issue and reflects the priorities of the government and the perceived objective of irrigation. It may be noted that in most countries, developed and developing, irrigation sector receives substantial subsidies from the Central Government. This is also the case where the irrigation agencies enjoy a high degree of financial autonomy. Typically, the subsidy involves a specified portion of the capital cost.[7] Decision on the nature and extent of subsidies is required to be taken in the context of choices made above.

Financial Autonomy and Physical Performance

Observations from other irrigation project points to a close linkage between their financial and physical performance. It has been argued (Small, 1989) that financially decentralised and autonomous organisations with a high degree of user involvement, exhibit better performance indicators. One of the potential advantages of decentralised financial autonomy is that it may create financial accountability linkages between the managers of irrigation projects and water users.[8]

> "In Mexico, where irrigation is also organised on the basis of decentralised financial autonomy, the financial linkage between user charges and funds for O & M appears to exert some degree of control over expenditure. Mexican farmers have reportedly stated that failure to operate the irrigation system in a cost-effective manner makes them unwilling to pay higher irrigation charges. It has also been noted in Mexico that in communally operated irrigation projects (i.e., irrigation units) where the water users are directly responsible for the conduct and financing of O & M, the maintenance is better than in government-run irrigation projects, where farmers have little involvement in expenditure control, other than the payment of water fees" (Small, 1989).

In an evaluation of a large number of irrigation projects, a World Bank study has noted that in general, the best irrigation performance was achieved in projects where: (1) the irrigation agencies themselves were responsible for the collection of the financial charges, and (2) the funds collected by the irrigation agencies remained with them for use in operating and maintaining the irrigation projects (Duane 1986). These are the key elements of financial autonomy.[9]

In all cases of financial autonomy, accountability by the agency to the users is ensured. Simultaneously, users institutionalised involvement ensures sharing a part of the responsibility for M&O. This entails a better communication and information flows between the two as opposed to the alienation observed when the users are totally divorced from any role in the M & O and creation of the irrigation systems. Labour contributions by users, for M & O of irrigation for example, would ensure better of work quality and prompt compliance and lower cash costs of M & O. Discussions of standardised per acre maintenance costs fixed in India thus would get suitably modified a welcome relief to the pressure on financial resources. Pressure to reduce wasteful expenditure due to constant social audit will bring further economies. However, the degree and form of user involvement, the demarcation of role of central agencies, their respective functions and areas of operation need to be delineated. While financial autonomy is planned for WUAs in the near future—its operationalisation in AP appears problematic in view of the inability to guarantee stipulated water deliveries. Aforementioned benefits from PIM may fail to come forth

End Use Regulation of Water

We have constantly emphasised above the need for on farm regulation of water for ensuring sustainability of the PIM programme in AP for the following reasons. As a result of irrigation reforms in the state water wastage due to *reduction of conveyance losses* has been cut down, thereby increasing the efficiency of water use at a macro level. The increased water availability due to this reduced wastage, however, can at best increase the water available for productive use by 20 to 25%. This increase can certainly make the water travel further down the channels—towards the tail end. But it is certainly not sufficient to travel to the tail end *and* provide multiple irrigation to tail end areas. For the latter to happen—it is absolutely necessary to *curtail* the amount of water being drawn upstream and divert it downstream. The total quantum of water is limited in the short run (on the average and with given hardware components). Increased water at the tail can make a significant impact *only* if it is made available *at the cost of upstream* farmers' i.e. by controlling their supply. That is, a drastic *re-distribution* of water is required. How this is envisaged in the overall programme is not clear. The redistribution implies the renunciation by the head end farmers of the disproportionate share of water that they have become accustomed to draw.

How is PIM in Andhra Pradesh going to effectively ground this redistribution in favour of tail end areas? By control structures? By persuasion and good will? Coercion? Who is going to take the politically unpalatable decisions of enforcing this reduction of water to head areas? It is well known that technical structures to control the water supplies have been tampered with earlier. Resistance to give up privileges enjoyed over the years is more likely to be offered. Conflict of economic interest is at the hard core of this resistance and farmers are acutely aware of this. The social injustice of head farmers' claim is not an issue of great concern to an individual head-end landowner. From visits to the field areas there is evidence of the tail-head issues being discussed in the Distributary Committees (DC) meetings. However, the DCs have no executive authority to implement the land based water distribution agreed to in principle or to take punitive action against those who violate the rules.

The PIM financial strategy was to stimulate revenue collection with higher water charges (recently hiked) by providing better service, such that the WUAs and DCs could be self-financing entities *vis-a-vis* the M & O works. The Rs. 200 per acre financial input matches to Rs. 200 per acre revenue collection. If the expected revenue collection is not forthcoming-the deficit has to be made up by outside sources. As of now it is the World Bank loans. However, loans have to be paid back and their flow is time bound. The question is—how do we pay back if there is a constant deficit and two—what happens when the inflow stops. The investments done in improving the supply network need to be kept up. If funds are not forthcoming for that—it will again set into motion the poor revenue—poor M & O—poor collections—poor

M & O ... cycle.

What then is the alternative? Are we trying to argue against the programme activities—is it futile? Is it to run down the admittedly useful revamping of the supply channels that was badly required? Such a position would no doubt be quite untenable. The argument is for carrying the process of irrigation reforms—which are necessary and inevitable—beyond the narrow confines of a supply side approach to include the critical realm of *end use regulation of water*. It is thus to take forward the process, which has been initiated, to its logical conclusion by bringing within its purview, the modes of *on farm utilisation of water, the cropping pattern and agricultural practices.* Using market and non-market interventions attempt should be made to influence choice of *low water consumption crops, water efficient technologies and adoption of agricultural practices, which enhance water productivity.*

There is no dearth of technological options available in the country. Hesitation is there, however, for expanding the mandate of PIM reforms to bring water-use within its fold. As of now the AP Farmers Act of 1996 very clearly states that the role of these reforms is to institute rules for equitable distribution of water (on per acre basis). What the farmers do with this water, is their business. As argued earlier, it is this aspect that can form the Achilles Heel of the entire programme. If rice cultivation is the only response of water users—the head reach farmers will continue to guzzle the water, starving the tail end farmers of their legitimate due. Real issues will get drowned in polemical discussions of 'water shortage'. Any attempt to cut into their water 'right' (by default due to years of grabbing) will be strongly countered. The entire investment at public cost would continue to cater to the privileged few, further reinforceing social and economic inequities, in addition to supporting low output agriculture.

The above calls for policy interventions—both market and non-market. We have noted later, the limitations of purely price-oriented policies. The successful impact of price interventions depends on the non-market environmental factors that allow a producer to avail of price concessions. For example, price support for inputs and outputs for stimulating the cultivation of low water intensive crop, should be accompanied by corresponding provision of technological extension, credit, input availability, access to output markets etc. The important point is that these inputs should converge on him *concurrently* for a focused support. Support that lacks co-ordination in time and space entails highly inefficient use of resources. While such packages are not yet available, it points to the future directions of research. Secondly, market interventions have a tendency to disproportionately favour the resource rich producers. To put it the other way round, market concessions do not discriminate on basis of resource position of consumers. Effort, therefore, has to be directed to focus non-market interventions specifically on the resource poor farmers to redress the imbalance in their socio-economic position.

People's Participation (PP)

People's Participation (PP) has of late acquired legitimacy in the policy circles. Recommending PP for implementation of various government programmes is fashionable and popular. However, there is less appreciation of the basic concept and the problems inherent in actualising PP. To begin with, the 'people' being talked about are not a homogeneous community or collective of individuals. They are divided into distinct categories based on socio-economic differences with conflicting interests. Any developmental intervention that has differential implications for different groups invokes differing responses from various social groups. Conflict resolution among competing interest groups constitutes the major challenge for PP. Typically, it is problematic for the state machinery to ground PP effectively, often for political reasons. Inputs from the NGO sector become crucial at this stage. Top-down approaches of the government require complementary grass-root efforts of the NGOs. This has been missing in the PIM programme in AP. Although NGOs have been involved at a secondary level of training etc., by and large the PIM is a top down approach instituted by government legislation and supported by government machinery. Conflict resolution at the grass-root level is, therefore, quite weak, which can defeat the objective of enlisting cooperative action for irrigation management.

It has been argued that uniformity of socio-economic conditions prevalent in a cooperative are more conducive for realising actual cooperation (Boyce, 1984; Wade, 1987; Sengupta, 1989; Jairath, 1989). Conversely, neutral rules of cooperation (for a perceived common benefit) among differentiated groups tend to reinforce the differentiation. Access to potential benefits of the scheme by the members of the collective is discriminatory. This constitutes a disincentive for cooperative effort by those who perceive the benefits as beyond their reach. Unless specific measures are taken to redress this imbalance, it discourages the reproduction of the cooperative spirit. It is in this context that the suggestion for a redistribution of small holdings in collective clusters as noted above (Rao, 1994), acquires significance, as this would improve the bargaining position of the small cultivators *vis-a-vis* the large farmers in the institutional framework of PIM. Hopeful of accessing benefits due to them, their cooperation is more likely to come forth. However, since the feasibility of redistributing land is doubtful, possibly the small holders could be organised into collectives for representing their specific interests.

Second point to reckon with is that PP does not refer to mere 'involvement' of the water users. The purpose of decentralisation is also to devolve decision-making powers. The acid test of effective devolution of decision-making authority is the ability to veto the decisions made beyond the people's organisations in case of conflict. There is some evidence of such happenings both by a recall of WUA member and protest against an uncooperative CA.[10]

Participation of the people in the initial stages has been very enthusiastic. Elections to WUAs were held on June 17, 1997. Although there was a financial incentive for holding unanimous of the office bearers, elections for nearly 40% of the WUAs were keenly contested. Conspicuous among the voters was the presence of women. Although the total number of eligible voters is less than that of men, since most of the land is in the name of the male head of the household, their turnout was proportionately higher. There were even some instances of women contesting for a member's position. They took an active part in the process of canvassing during the previous week. When interviewed, these women were very conscious and articulate about the objectives of the WUAs and their role as a member. This raises the issue of ensuring adequate representation for women in WUAs to offset their lower percentage as landowners. Their active participation in the elections and sensitivity to irrigation issues further strengthens the case. Thus, restricting the entry of women to WUA based on their non-ownership of land is unfortunate and amounts to reinforcing an existing deprivation. Possibly a dual membership—one male, one female—from each land owning family could be considered as a way of accommodating women as members of WUAs. However, this is an area that calls for a critical reassessment. Examples of eminently successful *women* presidents of WUA as noted during fieldwork further underscore the point. (See Box 7.1)

Alternative Paradigms

The foregoing discussion has been in the context of irrigation use of water. However, water has multiple uses and multiple sources that exist in nature in an integrated form. These sources are inter-linked and inter-dependent. Harnessing water for irrigation has repercussions on the other uses of water, apart from disturbing the total water balance in an area. While irrigation comprises a major proportion of water use in rural areas, other uses may be equally, if not more critical, inspite of requiring lower quantum. The most significant being the needs of safe and adequate drinking water. It is ironic to find unregulated drilling of borewells for irrigation in areas where hand pumps for drinking water are going dry due to declining water tables. Secondly, irrigation development caters only to the needs of the landowners/cultivators. It does not recognise the entitlements of the landless to the water resources of the area. Rights to water are inextricably linked to land. The land-linked privileges are further reinforced, accentuating the economic inequalities. Thirdly, ecological sustainability of water use patterns depends on an overall calculus of withdrawals and

Box 7.1

Dharma Sammakka

Pioneer of Women's Role in PIM

Dharma Sammakka from village Ellabotharam, in the command area of Kakatiya main canal of SRSP project in AP, is a live example of the capability and possibility of women playing an active role in PIM. She belies the arguments offered by most male farmers in the field, that PIM related activities are not suitable for women as it involves a lot of running around at odd hours. While safety and security of women are no doubt an issue of concern—there is nothing that women cannot 'manage', 'organise' and 'monitor' without violating the social norms. This fifty year old lady, who has passed 7th class in school, has a history of being involved in social development, work related to irrigation, women's credit groups, gram panchayat activities etc. In fact, she has been a member of gram panchayat nine years ago, when there was no special reservation for women.

Sammakka is the current president of Water User Association (WUA) No.3 (Ellabotharam) on D-89 distributary under SRSP project. She has fought this election and won against a male candidate. This is one of the very few WUAs, which have their own proper office which has all the basic data regarding the WUA portrayed in charts displayed on the walls. She is totally in command of the affairs of the WUA, which has 4 T.C. members, 589 general body members and an ayacut of 1151 acres and 11 gunthas. She had these detailed figures on her finger tips and was very specific about the numbers. It was in sharp contrast to a number of other WUA presidents interviewed, who either did not know the ayacut and the number of general body members of their WUA or were very vague and approximate about the figures.

Even her record maintenance was extensive and up to date—she maintained 17 registers, held regular general body and managing committee meetings, recorded the minutes and attendance etc. Among the works undertaken and contemplated by their WUA was the de-silting of channels, installing of shutters, strengthening of embankments and painting of gauges. She claimed a modest increase of 10 acres in area irrigated due to WUA efforts, but mentioned that water supply was more certain now.

She had personally made a number of visits to the Pay and Accounts Office in Karimnagar to pursue the release of funds, was in active contact with the Competent Authority, personally conducted and presided over the managing committee meetings. She had full support of her husband (a retired school teacher) for her public activities. In fact, her only son and husband was very proud of her role in social affairs—but never interfered in her work or acted as her proxies.

Illustration as above point to the need to give a greater prominence to gender issue in PIM and facilitate women's involvement—which is not only possible and successful, but also necessary for gender equity. This is particularly critical since, by and large, women do not own the land and this discrimination would be partially offset by recognising their rights to water—and their say in its proper use and management.

available recharges. Irrigation planning by different sources cannot be done independent of total water resource planning. Irrigation needs, therefore, have to be subsumed under overall demands on water resources for satisfying requirements of balanced development. Planning of irrigation has, therefore, to carried out as a part and parcel of water resources planning. This calls for a change of paradigm from irrigation management to *Integrated Water Resource Management (IWRM)*. PIM, therefore, has to be replaced by participatory *water* management i.e. PWM.

In consonance with IWRM, patterns of water use in the canal commands also should follow *watershed-based approach*. There is need to conserve and regulate water use in command areas of irrigation projects as well for sustainable exploitation of water sources. This is in line with our thesis posited above on the need for end use regulation of water and ecological sustainability of water related interventions that require an integrated perspective. The need for water conservation in irrigation commands is not yet a part of irrigation policy formulation.

Recent researches[11] within this viewpoint have proposed alternative technical approaches to water use that enable higher input efficiencies by controlling water applications to the crop root zone during critical period of plant growth. The criteria of water technology choice would be its capacity to minimise unproductive evaporation from soil surface as well as water bodies and reduce conveyance losses. Concurrently it would minimise energy and energy intensive inputs, thus reducing financial burden on the users. This method is labour intensive, use locally available materials such as low cost/energy alternatives to sprinkler/drip irrigation. (Water Technologies, 1998).

Remarkable improvements in water use efficiency have been realised through close control on the quantum and timing of water application and soil improvement by use of organic inputs. Much of nutrients and water are wasted in surface irrigation as water is applied to entire surface area. The extent of active root zone can be limited by selective soil improvement, by organic matter applied to localised root development. Prof. Dhabolkar's experiments have successfully used these methods to record productivity of 40-60 kgs/hamm of water compared to 25-35 kgs/hamm by conventional methods. Using these techniques it has been possible to create food security for a family of five on a land holding of only 10 gunthas with requiring 2M³ water per day.

The approach is in contrast to the high input system, where most of the experimental work is done in the experimental farms and is relevant to the well endowed areas and resourceful farmers, who have access to unrestricted water and chemical inputs. Further, it is a very effective means of integrating the local indigenous knowledge based on years of experience of the producers in the specific locale with the expertise of the professional.

Finally, extensive cultivation possible with efficient and conservative use of water has the potential of supporting biomass production for feeding bio-based units of electricity generation at the local level. Experiments have already been conducted in Karnataka by ASTRA, Bangalore. See also Datye (1997). This is particularly relevant in the context of an undulating terrain found in the peninsular region that requires energy for pumping of water for delivery to fields. These ideas have the potential for local self-reliance of energy, which can be used to obtain water for ensuring their basic livelihood needs. Linking energy with water use pattern can spin off multiple benefits in the rural areas, particularly among the economically weaker classes.

NOTES

1. S.N. Singh, 2000, Personal Communication.
2. *See state expenditure in budget documents discussed in Jairath (1999) report for the RBI.*
3. D. V. Vaish at UNICEF, Hyderabad, developed this categorisation with reference to maintenance of hand pumps for drinking water. See Vaish (1998).
4. *According to the estimates made by the Public Accounts Committee, the total losses from irrigation works were found to have increased from Rs. 1,550 million in 1975-76 to Rs. 4,050 million in 1980-85 and Rs. 6,600 million in 1984-85). Not only that very often costs of fee collection are very high. In Bihar for instance, fee collected, as a proportion of M & O costs measure of financial efficiency, is higher than fee collected (Bhatia, 1989, p 235). While in Korea, combination of high fees and high rate of collection enables the farmers to pay 98 per cent of M & O cost.* (Small, 1989).

5. More than 50% of the area in the state is irrigated under major and medium irrigation by canals followed by 35% under tubewells and 15% under tanks.
6. See Water Pricing (1992/94) and Vaidyanathan for a review of the recommendations of the Commission on water prices to the GOI.
7. In France, for instance, the subsidies cover 20-60% of capital cost. In addition, an implicit subsidy exists in the form of low interest loans to repay the balance capital cost. Similar arrangements are found in Taiwan/Korea and Japan (Small, 1989).
8. *It is reported, for example, that irrigation districts in China, unlike most economic enterprises in the state sector, are not overstaffed. The reason given for this is that the arrangement whereby the revenue of the district comes from the water users provides an incentive to limit the number of personnel (Nickum 1982:22). There is also evidence that water users in China use the threat of non-payment of water fees as a means of leverage over management* (Nickum 1982:38).
9. "In Taiwan, it appears that the method of financing is such that the managers of the irrigation associations face an incentive structure, which encourages them to manage the system efficiently. This is partly due to the financial autonomy of the irrigation associations, and the resulting importance of high rates of fee collection to preserve the jobs of the staff of the irrigation associations .... farmers in one irrigation association who felt they were not receiving good service responded by withholding payments. The fact that such an action was taken, and that it apparently led to subsequent actions to improve service, resulting in very high levels of payments a few years later, suggests that the financial accountability associated with the financing mechanism used in Taiwan has a positive effect on the efficiency of management performance" (Small, 1989).
10. See report in Deccan Chronicle dated May 25, 1999, which mentions the action taken against CAs in response to the complaints by farmers of villages Mukhetswaram and Malikipuram.
11. The experiments entailed providing nursery soil to create required productive root zone volume in relation to the canopy area. The soil should have adequate organic matters and moisture holding capacity as well as sufficiently high rate of infiltration. The micronutrients are obtained from recycling of waste. Observing composition of the ash content of the plant component produced at various stages assesses the requirement of micronutrients according to the growth stages especially of phosphorus. The mineral nutrient waste is minimised as they are applied at appropriate growth stage. These principles provide the framework by *self-evaluation* of performance on the basis of observing the dry matter production during various growth stages of the plant and final output. The knowledge exchange helps to raise the capabilities of the experimenter. The system becomes widely replicable by soil improvement and recycling waste and makes productive utilisation of local labour possible at all stages, including initial stages of development of land and plantation and as well as later, of sustaining the production with minimum of external input (Water Technologies, 1998).

8

CONCLUDING COMMENTS

To sum up the observations, we have noted above the upsurge of activity in the irrigated commands initiated as a result of implementing reforms to institute participation of water users for the management of irrigation systems. More than 10,000 organisations have been created with clearly specified mandate, responsibilities and powers in the legal enactment. There is overwhelming evidence for the repairs and rehabilitation work done throughout the state and spread over different projects. Heavy inflow of funds has been injected through these organisations of water users which have in fact been utilised for what they were earmarked. Dispersed works of smaller scale and concurrent activity in this direction has served to discourage leakage that is typically associated with the conduct of physical works in the irrigation sector. The establishment of the entire structure of participatory institutions and with enabling capacity to initiate action is indeed commendable for a state initiated programme and speaks volumes of the political will and determination to push through the programme.

It would indeed be a tragedy if this dynamic initiative for revolutionising the management of water use for agriculture is short lived. The experience is being watched the world over and the lurking apprehension at the back of everyone's mind is—How sustainable will be the reforms. The expectations and stakes are high. The key question therefore is—how do we ensure the self-reliance of these atomic WUAs, which are the building blocks of PIM institutions in AP.

One of the necessary conditions–although by no means sufficient by itself—for sustainable reproduction of WUAs as viable entities is their financial self-sufficiency. We have pointed how critical this is for the successful entrenchment of PIM institutions in Mexico. That this is problematic under the present system of an overwhelming priority for using water for rice by the cultivators in almost all the commands has also been argued above. Monopolisation of water by the head reach farmers inspite of increased availability as a result of improvement in physical structures confines the benefit to relatively smaller number of farmers. This discourages the payment of water cess by the downstream farmers as a matter of right, while the head end farmers are also defaulting on their payments inspite of getting more than their due share of water, even during water scarcity period. This reduces the financial inflows required for recurring expenses to maintain the system in a functional state over the years. This will set into motion the cycle of poor upkeep leading to loss of functionality and consequent dampening of expectations of a section of water users from the system. Such a situation weakens the hold of participatory institutions.

Rice is a highly water intensive crop. It is the only attractive option in soils with high moisture content in many areas. It also constitutes the food crop in the region. While growing rice may be necessary on a portion of the command, its extensive cultivation as currently practiced cannot be explained as above. In fact, this has been made possible only due to a total breakdown in the rules of water distribution and regulation that has ensured unbridled access to water by water users at the head of main canal, distributaries and minors. Unless the PIM reforms can bring about significant control over water distribution, not only is the situation likely to continue, paradoxically enough it may worsen. Enforcing compliance to rules of water distribution by the establishment will be unpopular and cannot be expected to happen on account of political imperatives. Social pressure of WUAs on each other does not have the "teeth" required for insisting on adherence to the code of water sharing agreed upon. Financial incentive is sought to be offered to the WUAs for enhancing water fee collections in their commands. This will be futile in the absence of effective water regulation. Secondly, even where the water is available, there are limitations of the control of WUAs over its general body members. We have pointed out the weak links of the user representatives with the electorate. This constrains their ability to effect higher collections as well as monitor unauthorised withdrawals of water from the channels that must pass through their lands for carrying water to downstream cultivators. Moreover, higher collections are an incentive only for the members of WUA, as they control the funds, not so much for the members of general body.

Given the above scenario, it is imperative to include the realm of water use within the fold of PIM reforms or other policy intervention. Effective strategies are required to be worked out for weaning the farmers away from cultivation of water intensive crops such as rice. AP has been called the "rice bowl" of the country. Living upto the image can be costly blunder. There are already reports of over production of rice in the country, which are rotting in the FCI godowns (Omvedt, 1999). Clearly the macro considerations dictate a shift to less water consumption cropping package. The point is to influence micro level decisions of an individual producer to favour less water demanding crops and practices by interventions geared to induce changes in his environment. The above calls for market and non-market interventions. We have also noted the limitations of purely price-oriented policies. The successful impact of price interventions depends on the non-market environmental factors that allow a producer to avail of price concessions.

The final argument is for carrying the process of irrigation reforms—which are necessary and inevitable—beyond the narrow confines of a supply side approach to include the critical realm of end use regulation of water. It is thus to take forward the process, which has been initiated, to its logical conclusion by bringing within its purview, the modes of on farm utilisation of water, the cropping pattern and agricultural practices.

This has corresponding implications for research agenda for the PIM fraternity. In the context of AP, one of the key questions to be investigated is the reason underlying the strong preference for water intensive cultivation and resistance to less water consumptive and/or high economic return cropping pattern. Issues of technological change in agriculture and impediments to technological diffusion and absorption need to be explored.

APPENDIX I

WATER PRICING

Unlike free market price determination, price of water requires to be fixed by government dictate. This has always been a point of debate and discussion. The criteria and level of price fixation have been the contentious issues. It has been argued that water charges for irrigation from public sources have been fixed at very low level relative to the output possible with its use and relative to the cost of production. Alternatively, it has been posited that if the secondary benefits of irrigation are taken into account due to the multiplier effect initiated by irrigation investment in an area, the net benefits from irrigation far outweigh the costs. There is thus an outflow from irrigation to the treasury (Bhatia, 1989, Vaidyanathan, 1998). Even if there are net outflows from irrigation sector, one cannot overlook the fact that the output (in terms of productivity levels actually attained) are not commensurate with the investments made to create the irrigation potential. The fundamental problem however remains one of institutional mismanagement leading to poor physical output and wastage of financial resources. While arguments for raising the water rates may mis-perceive the problem, those who argue against the need for it may generate complaicance not warranted by ground level realities. The issue is complex and cannot be reduced to cost considerations sans extent and quality of output.

Since most of the public irrigation is through canals, the issue is generally discussed with reference to canal irrigation. To begin with high cost of canal irrigation is emphasised in contrast to low water rates prevalent, especially in the context of the benefits of enhanced yields accruing to the farmers. The implication thereby is to argue for increasing the rates. The context of discussion, however, remains imprisoned within a commercial calculus and points to the irrationality of selling below what it 'costs'. These 'costs of production' referred to subsume within them the leakage and inefficiencies typically associated with most public irrigation projects (see Jairath, 1999a for detailed evidence in case of AP). As a basis for assessing the relative benefits, therefore, these costs are clearly inadequate.

Secondly, high or low cost has to have reference to the quality of commodity produced. i.e. irrigation supplied to the farmers in this case. Selling price does not drive its rationale from cost considerations alone. The market for the commodity with quality specifications has to exist. Demand side considerations of the utility of irrigation to the user and the effectiveness with which is in fact, available to the farmer are pertinent points for assessing the level of water charges. Given the wide-ranging evidence on poor conditions of provision of canal irrigation, discussed extensively in the recent literature on institutional aspects of irrigation, there is reason to doubt the validity of the 'low water rates' hypotheses. Low water rates with respect to what? Production costs? What about production inefficiencies? Do we argue for raising the rates to cover up these inefficiencies and expect the water users to pay the price? Or do we investigate the reasons for the same and attempt to institute measures to streamline the entire process of creation and under-utilisation of irrigation? Operating at the level of financial arguments to the exclusion of underlying realities of production can be a misleading basis of policy formulation. Although couched in terms of subsidies—it can be characterised more aptly as a slick marketing strategy for selling poor quality irrigation at a throw away price.

Thirdly, it is ironic that the issue of raising water rates is brought up in the light of extremely poor collection rates typically witnessed in the country. Very often the costs of collection of these water charges are higher than the total fee collected (Bhatia, 1989). If such is the situation with low water rates, higher rates *per se* can make little difference to the revenue of the irrigation department. The rationally motivated farmer may simply refuse to buy water if it is not 'worth' the price. Enforcement is not politically viable.

In this context, it has been argued that subsidised water tends to encourage wasteful use. Higher prices, would, therefore, be instrumental for more judicious use of water, as discussed above. The above raises the broader issue of using water *pricing as a lever for influencing water use and cropping patterns.* The inclination and incentive of the user to pay for irrigation is contingent on what he is getting for the money. The reluctance to pay even the admittedly low water rates is rooted in the mistrust between the farmer and the agency in charge of supplying water. The farmer has no control over the rigid and uncertain irrigation through canals. This leaves little operational flexibility in his hands to optimally use the available water for coping up with multiple uncertainties inherent in agricultural production.

The farmers' capacity and inclination to pay the water charges follow, *inter alia,* from the provision of adequate irrigation in terms of the reliability and controllability of water supplies. In fact, willingness to pay higher charges may well come forth, provided they are assured of superior service of irrigation.[1] It has been widely observed in other developing countries also that the water users are less sensitive to price of irrigation than to its 'adequacy' or suitability for given production requirements.[2] *Therefore, it is not low water charges that entail inefficient use of irrigation but inefficient irrigation that results in low collection of low water charges.* The strategy should, therefore, be not only to raise the rates, which by itself will be futile. Rather the attempt should be to provide efficient and predictable irrigation with user control over the timing and quantum. Evidence from different parts of the world points to the fact that effective institutionalising participatory mechanisms irrigation management have led to higher collection rates inspite of higher contributions for M&O by the farmers. Further, the quality of maintenance was distinctly superior to that of publicly managed systems (Small, 1989).

Finally, it may be noted that the poor quality of irrigation supplied through canals is partially compensated for the larger farmers who receive water in a lump sum. Economies of scale, their privileged social position and the political clout that goes with it, enable the large farmers to neutralise supply side bottlenecks to a significant extent. The discriminatory advantage of low water rates is in fact available to them as they control a larger chunk of the command area under irrigation projects. However, they are also the ones who have access to alternative and more efficient forms of irrigation such as tubewells, provided they are technologically feasible. The attraction of canals for them is correspondingly diminished. Raising water rates without corresponding improvements in quality may give a further impetus to switching away from canals altogether, thus reinforcing the existing underutilisation of irrigation potential created through canals.

The point is that tinkering with the level of water rates may lead to paradoxical consequences. Disincentive to use canals may lead to lower utilisation and still lower returns. However, this is not to argue that the water rates should not be increased. Higher water charges should be compared with the higher profitability made possible with high value input. If increased returns with better quality irrigation can more than makeup for high costs of irrigation, there would, in fact, be no political resistance to increasing water rates. This may not only be required but also become feasible provided radical steps are taken to improve supply side efficiencies. This is no doubt being done in AP with tremendous zeal and financial backing, as discussed above. The major limitation, however, is that success is noticeably confined to technical streamlining of the irrigation projects. Although, institutional reforms are an integral component of the PIM strategy in AP, its effective implementation may be constrained due to political problems associated with ensuring equitable distribution of available irrigation supplies. The given quantum of water resources in the state is an 'elastic' magnitude can be made to 'expand' and provide irrigation to a larger area and more cultivators, provided a concerted effort is made to wean the farming community away from an obsession with rice cultivation. Issue of 'water scarcity' is, therefore, partly an artificial construct. The transition to alternative water use trajectory requires attempts to regulate end use of water.

NOTES

1. Clear evidence for this is provided by the switch from canals to tubewells witnessed in some of the most productive regions of the country (Jairath, 1998). The distinct preference for tubewells, which are a costlier proposition than canals (where the cost to the user is negligible), counters the widely held view that farmers are not inclined to pay their dues irrespective of what they receive.
2. For some World Bank projects in Sri Lanka it was found that in case of the first few irrigation schemes the farmers failed to adopt irrigation even though they paid low or non-existent charges for irrigation. However, in a sixth project farmers paid $50 per hectare per season and immediately used irrigation water and continued to use it at a high rate. (World Bank, 1981).

Bibliography

Act, 1997, Andhra Pradesh Farmers Management of Irrigation Systems Act,.GOAP, Hyderabad.

Action Plan 1995, Action Plan for Completion of Irrigation Projects, Irrigation and CAD Department.

Bandhopadhyay, N. K. 1992, Brief Note on Selection of Sites and Transfer of M. I. Installations under West Bengal Minor Irrigation Project to Beneficiaries Through Panchayat Samities, in Bandhopadhayay, N. K. Review of Proposals of Government of Maharashtra for passing the O&M of Irrigation Canals below the minors to the group of farmers, report to the World Bank.

Bhatia, R. 1989, Financing Irrigation Services in India – A Case Study of Bihar and Haryana States in Small *et al.*, 1989.

Boyce, J. 1988, Technological and Institutional Alternatives in Asian Rice Irrigation, Economic and Political Weekly, Vol. XXIII, No. 13, March 26, pp A-6 to A-22.

Brewer, J *et al.* 1998, Irrigation Management Transfer in India–Policies, Processes and Performance, a collaborative study by IIM, Ahmedabad, India and IIMI, Colombo, Sri Lanka.

Brewer, J. *et al.* (IIM & IIMI) 1998, Irrigation Management Transfer in India: Policies, Processes & Performance, A Collaborative Study by Indian Institute of Management, Ahmedabad, India and IIMI, Colombo, Sri Lanka.

CASAD/SOPPECOM/SARMET 1998, An Integrated Perspective for Energy Generation and Utilisation, December, Mumbai.

Datye, K. R. (Assisted by Suhas Paranjpe and K. J. Joy) 1997, Banking on bio-mass—A new strategy for sustainable prosperity based on renewable energy and dispersed industrialisation, Environment and Development Series, Centre for Environment Education, Ahmedabad.

DIPR 1999. From a Drop to an Ocean, *The Hindu,* 24th May.

Doorknobs, J. and Kasan, A. H. 1997, Yield Response to Water, FAO Irrigation and Drainage Papers # 33.

Factual Note 1996, Irrigation Sector: A Factual Note, GOAP, Irrigation and CAD Department, Hyderabad.

Feedback 1998 & 1999, Analysis of WUA Presidents Feedback obtained in the Sadassus held in Hyderabad and Vijayawada, April, CAD, GOAP.

Jairath, J. 1989, Inequity and Resources Use Efficiency, Mimeo, National Institute of Science Technology and Development Studies, Delhi.

Jairath, J. 1999a, Status Report of Irrigation in AP, Center for Economic and Social Studies (CESS), Hyderabad.

Jairath, J. 1999b, Participatory Irrigation Management in Andhra Pradesh, *Economic and Political Weekly* (EPW), Vol. XXXIV, No. 40, Oct. 2.

Jairath, J. 1985, Technical and Institutional Factors in Utilisation of Irrigation – A Case of Public Canals in Punjab, *Economic and Political Weekly* Vol. XX, No. 13, March 30, pp A-2 to A-10.

Johnson, S. H. & others 1997, Impact Assessment of Irrigation Management Transfer in the Alto Rio Lerma Irrigation District, Mexico, Research Report No. 15, International Irrigation Management Institute (IIMI), Sri Lanka.

Johnson, S. H. & others 1997, Irrigation Management Transfer in Mexico: A Strategy to Achieve Irrigation District Sustainability, Research Report No. 16, IIMI, Sri Lanka.

Jurriens, M. and Landstra, W. 1989, Water Distribution: Conflicting Objectives of Scheme Management and Farmers, ILRI reprint No. 58, Wageningen, The Netherlands

Meinzen-Dick, R. 1997, Towards New Partnerships in Indian Irrigation, Paper presented at workshop on PIM in India, New Delhi, Jan 20th.

Ministers Statement 1998, Gap in irrigation potential bridged, *The Hindu,* Dec. 16th.

Mollinga, P. 1998, On the Waterfront–Water distribution, technology and agrarian change in a South Indian Canal Irrigation System, Ponsen en Looijen, Wageningen, The Netherlands.

Nickum, J. E. 1979, The Organisation of water resource development in the People's Republic of China. *Agricultural Administration,* July, 169-186.

Note on the ACT, 1997, Note on Andhra Pradesh Farmers' Management of Irrigation Systems Act, for District Collectors' Conference, Irrigation & CAD, Department, Hyderabad.

Omvedt, G. 1999, Rotting Food, *The Hindu* Oct. 23rd.

Pathak, R. S. 1991, Farmers, Participation in Irrigation Water Management, Ministry of Water Resources, New Delhi.

Pricing Report 1992/94 Report of the Committee on Pricing of Irrigation Water: Government of India, Planning Commission, New Delhi, September 1992

Pundarikanthan, N. V. *et al.* 1992, Main System Performance and Management Control Processes: Tambarpani System in Proceedings of the workshop on IIMI – India Collaborative Research in Irrigation Management, IIMI, Colombo, Sri Lanka.

Rao, CHH 1994, Agricultural Growth: Rural Poverty and Environmental Degradation in India, OUP, Delhi.

Reddy, D. N. 1999, Designer Participation: Politics of Irrigation Management Reforms in Andhra Pradesh—India, Paper submitted to the International Researcher's Conference on Participatory Irrigation Management at Hyderabad, India, 11-14 December.

Sengupta, N. 1989, Irrigation Policy and Irrigation Associations, Madras Institute of Development Studies, Chennai

Small, L. E. *et al.* 1989, Financing Irrigation Services: A Literature Review and selected Case Studies from Asia, IIMI, Colombo, Sri Lanka.

Srivastava, L. P. and Brewer, J. D. 1994 Irrigation Management Transfer at Paliganj, Bihar, India. Short Report Series on Locally Managed Irrigation No. 7, IIMI, Colombo, Sri Lanka.

TH, 1999, 5.12 lac acre of land benefited from irrigation works: Tummala, *The Hindu,* March 15th.

TH, 1998, Irrigation Official Suspended, *The Hindu,* May 25th.

UNICEF, 1997, Income and Expenditure Pattern of Gram Panchayats, UNICEF & PRED, Hyderabad.

Vaidyanathan, A. 1998, Political Economy of Water Pricing, Paper presented at workshop on Alternative Approaches to Canal Irrigation Reforms in India, held at Hyderabad, 18th to 22nd December.

Vaish, D. P. 1998, Community Ownership: Key to Effective Hand Pump Maintenance in Proceedings of State Level Workshop, Rural Water Supply & Sanitation, 26-27 April, Hyderabad, India.

Venkateshwarlu, D. 1999, Politics of Irrigation Management Reforms in Andhra Pradesh, Paper submitted to the International Researcher's Conference on Participatory Irrigation Management at Hyderabad, India, 11-14 December.

Vermillion, D. L. 1997, Impacts of Irrigation Management Transfer: A review of evidence, Report No. 11, International Irrigation Management Institute (IIMI), Colombo, Sri Lanka.

Wade, R. 1987, *Village Republics,* CUP & Orient Longman.

Wade, R. 1987, The Management of Common Property Resources: Collective action as an alternative to privatisation or state regulation, *Cambridge Journal of Economics,* Vol. II, No. 2, pp, 95-106.

Water Technologies, 1998, CASAD/ SOPPECOM, Mumbai, December.

World Bank, 1981, Water Management in Bank supported irrigation project systems: An analysis of past experience. Operation Evaluation Department, Report 3421, Washington DC, USA.

INDEX